Peter Mason was born in Australia, but has lived in since 1959. He started work at the age of sixteen as a copy-boy with United Press International, and since then has worked as a newspaper reporter, agency sub-editor, motoring writer, radio journalist and public relations man. He was named Reporter of the Year in the 1980 British Press Awards for his reporting of the Iranian Embassy siege in London.

His chief interests outside journalism are travel and dangerous sports in which he indulges himself to the full. He is a keen sailor and windsurfer, hang-glider pilot, parachutist, scuba-diver and hot air balloonist.

He lives by the sea in Kent with his English wife, Sheila, and two sons.

John Burns is also a journalist. Born in Belfast, he worked on several local newspapers. He became the only provincial journalist ever to win the New Reporter of the Year award—for his coverage of the Ulster troubles. Armed with this title, and a singularly tacky presentation desk set, he moved to London ten years ago to seek his fortune. He is still looking.

He lives with his wife, Rita, and two young sons in Finchley.

Also by Peter Mason

THE BOOK OF NARROW ESCAPES
and published by Corgi Books

Peter Mason and John Burns

The Book of
Criminal Blunders

Illustrated by

McLACHLAN

CORGI BOOKS

THE BOOK OF CRIMINAL BLUNDERS
A CORGI BOOK   0 552 12654 3

First publication in Great Britain

PRINTING HISTORY
Corgi edition published 1985

This book is set in 10/11 pt Plantin

Corgi Books are published by Transworld Publishers Ltd.,
Century House, 61–63 Uxbridge Road, Ealing, London W5 5SA,
in Australia by Transworld Publishers (Aust.) Pty. Ltd.,
26 Harley Crescent, Condell Park, NSW 2200, and in New
Zealand by Transworld Publishers (N. Z.) Ltd., Cnr. Moselle
and Waipareira Avenues, Henderson, Auckland.

Made and printed in Great Britain by
Hunt Barnard Printing Ltd., Aylesbury, Bucks.

Acknowledgements

The authors would like to express their sympathy and condolences to all the victims whose sorry tales are recounted herein, together with their gratitude to all those who helped in the compilation of THE BOOK OF CRIMINAL BLUNDERS. Special thanks to Maurice Dodd, Peter Muller, Richard Jones and Mike Braham, and to our many friends and colleagues in Fleet Street and elsewhere who came to our aid with their own tales of the sublime and the ridiculous, without which this book would not have been possible. Thanks, too, to our wives, Sheila and Rita, for help with typing, research and endless cups of coffee.

List of Contents

The authors would like to point out that the details and circumstances of the blunders, bloomers, criminal cock-ups and assorted felonies recounted in this volume are all indisputably, undeniably, absolutely, perfectly true. They have, however, taken the precaution of changing some of the names to protect the guilty, not to mention themselves.

The authors would also like to point out that whilst there appears to be a heavy preponderance of Irish blunders in these pages, they have nothing against the Irish. On the contrary, and lest the killjoys of the Socialist Republic of Islington feel tempted to ban this tome from their library shelves, not only is one of the authors Irish, but his mother came from Ireland too!

Anyway, Irishmen, in court, are like DC10 airliners: you only hear about the ones that crash.

Foreword

History has for decades held a special place for that elite club of criminals who can execute a crime so cunningly that they confound even the most dedicated detective.

For even in the underworld of outlaws, crooks and villains, there are those who succeed against all the odds. The shrewd, the sly, the cagey and the brilliant, heroes all who, like the infamous Raffles, win the admiration of all but their unfortunate victims in the masterful execution of their crimes.

And then there are the others.

For every successful criminal there is the buffoon counterpart—the bungling burglar, the hopeless house-breaker, the muddle-headed mugger. The ne'er do-wells who turn to crime because they're no good at anything else, only to find that they're no good at crime either.

They are the thieves who drop their wallets in the middle of the bedroom they've just burgled, or climb into broken-down getaway cars that splutter and die at the most untimely moment . . . the bank robbers who write hold-up notes on the back of their bank deposit slips, complete with name and address . . . the flashers who get their trousers caught round their ankles and stumble into the waiting arms of the police.

The hopeless, hapless felons whose biggest crime is incompetence, and on whom the worst sentence that can be passed by their peers, or meted out to them by the judge, is the humiliation that comes from being caught.

Imagine the shame of one would-be master criminal, a bungler beyond belief, on being told by the judge: 'You're a rotten burglar—always in trouble and always being caught. You may as well give up. You are a disgrace to your profession.'

Or the embarrassment of the Irishman who, after walking into a garden supply shop and asking for change for a tenner, snatched a £5 note from the open till and ran out the door—leaving his own £10 note on the counter.

Before setting off on his escapade of discovery, and mindful of the need to minimise the risk of prosecution afterwards, he wrote letters to his solicitor, the bank manager, and, of course, the police. Then, armed with an imitation revolver, he burst into the bank and shouted: 'Everyone freeze – this is a hold-up.' At which point one of the tellers, who had not yet been apprised of the plot, whipped out a gun and shot him dead.

Of course, it's not always the criminal who gets it wrong. Often it's the law that shows itself up to be an even bigger ass than the villains against whom it is supposed to be protecting society.

Judge Peter Slot once allowed a defendant in a burglary trial to leave the courtroom to feed his parking meter. The man disappeared.

And Old Bailey judge Michael Argyle sparked off quite a controversy when he freed a man who tore the clothes off a top model, tried to rape her, banged her head on the floor, slapped her face, and then tried to throttle her by grabbing her round the throat.

The judge told the man: 'You come from Derby, which is my part of the country. Now off you go and don't come back.'

That momentary lapse in good jugement nearly cost the judge his job, and earned him the dubious title 'the rapist's friend'.

There were no accolades, either, for the police who decided to prosecute a 50 year-old grandmother for shoplifting, only to have the case thrown out in court when it was discovered that she had stolen her own gloves.

Of course, there's no reason to assume that judges, lawyers and policemen should be any less susceptible to the temptations of the flesh than the rest of us.

Even Lord Chief Justices have fallen foul of the law over the years, some of them turning out to be criminal rogues of the first order.

Elizabeth I's Lord Chief Justice, John Popham, was a one-time mugger and highwayman. Another, Thomas Parker, fell from grace in 1725 when he was fined £30,000 for fraud – a princely sum in those days – and spent six weeks incarcerated in the Tower of London.

But don't let *us* spoil you with the details. Let the blunderers speak for themselves.

We will leave you to read on with the words of Horace ringing in your ears . . . .

'It is grievous to be caught.'

The Good, The Bad . . . And The Downright Unlucky

The case histories we are about to relate just go to prove the truth of the Great Banana Skin Theory: in short, no matter who you are, you're just as likely as the next man to end up flat on your backside with a silly grin on your face and four red cheeks.

Take the Good; the decent law-abiding citizen who treads Life's straight and narrow, his eyes fixed on Higher Things, heedless of the peril underfoot, until . . . WHOOPS!

Or, again, the Bad; the wayward soul on the slippery slope, largely paved with his own peelings.

And then there's the Downright Unlucky; the chap so anxious not to step on the cracks in the pavement that he puts his foot right on the old banana.

Laugh at them if you dare.

The Good the Bad ... and the Downright Unlucky

Inside job

Roy Whaley thought he was seeing things when a gunman burst in on him and shouted: 'This is a robbery. We're taking all your stuff.'

For Whaley, a convicted robber, was in his prison cell at the time – and the gunman had broken *in*to the jail at Pompano Beach, Florida, to carry out the bizarre raid.

As Whaley and cellmate Mark Burwitz watched openmouthed, the man scooped up a stereo, an expensive radio, a television set, an alarm clock, a gold watch and $30 in cash. Then he fled.

The inside-out intruder was later identified as a convict who had gone over the wall two months earlier.

Officials described the hold-up as 'ironic'. Said prison superintendent Barry Ahringer: 'If you're not safe in prison where the hell are you safe?'

Miss-taken identity

As a big shot in the community, the police chief of Leganes, near Madrid, claimed the first kiss from the fiesta beauty queen. But just as he stepped forward to embrace the newly-crowned lovely, he recognised the winner as a local transvestite. The chief didn't get his kiss. But then he/she didn't get the title either.

A fair cop

Police constable Fiona Melaniphy was a fair cop, and so was flasher Michael Biggs' arrest following an incident in a London pub.

Biggs, a kitchen porter, was caught with his trousers down – literally – when he exposed himself to the shapely brunette, who promptly nicked him.

In court, charged with indecent exposure, Biggs apologised to PC Melaniphy, who was in plain clothes at the time of his arrest. Said Biggs: 'I didn't dream, looking at your legs and figure, that you could possibly be a policewoman.'

Forgive us our trespassers

While the Reverend Simon Beesley was chairing a meeting called to discuss the growing burglary problem in his parish, two burglars rifled the bedroom of his vicarage in Roby, Merseyside, and made off with the contents.

Blind man's bluff

Would-be bank robber David Rich couldn't see the joke when everyone started laughing at him. He couldn't see very much at all, what with *three* stocking masks plus a thick scarf covering his face.

Thus disguised he stumbled and fumbled his way through the doors of the NatWest branch at Cricklewood, North London.

Haltingly he made his way to the counter where he ordered customers and staff to lie on the floor or he would shoot.

To show he meant business, Rich stuck his hand in his pocket, and produced . . . his spectacles case. Staff fell about in stitches as he threatened to pull the trigger and at last Rich, sensing that something had gone wrong, made a run for it.

It wasn't a very fast run, on account of his disguise, and he had to rip off the masks, one by one, as he fled.

Police arriving on the scene within moments followed the trail and found him cowering behind a parked car.

Rich, 27, told them: 'I just wanted to be rich.'

The Government was strongly urged to take steps to put a stop to the growing evil of methylated spirit drinking by the Liverpool justices at their quarterly meetings. – **From a report in a Liverpool newspaper**

The sweet smell of failure

Customs officers at Dover smelt a rat when the man from the Mafia pulled up in his sparkling Mercedes.

Never before had a car radiated such fragrant odours. Convinced they were hot on the scent of an international perfume smuggler, the excise men swooped.

But under a heap of air fresheners they found Ernesto

Marifa's real contraband – a £150,000 cannabis consignment stashed in a secret compartment.

Ernesto, from Palermo, Sicily, lamely explained he had piled the car with air fresheners to put sniffer dogs off the scent. He is serving five years.

Gift rap

Derek 'Poddy' Podmore thought he'd play a little Christmas joke on the governor of his local prison.

He'd already earned a certain amount of notoriety in his home town of Shrewsbury by climbing the prison walls dressed as Santa Claus and throwing cigarettes to the inmates. This time he needed something with a little more, well . . . ooomph!

So he wired up an alarm clock to a sinister looking electrical circuit and attached it to two green candles; the big ones that look at first glance like gelignite. Then he parcelled it all up and took it down to the post office.

Somewhat perturbed by the appearance of the parcel, postal sorters alerted police who duly called in an Army bomb disposal squad.

After cordoning off the street outside they carefully prised open the parcel and dismantled the 'bomb'. Inside they found a note which said: 'Start Christmas with a bang.'

In court, charged with sending a dummy explosive to Mr Stephen Pryor, the prison governor, Poddy, who was described somewhat whimsically as 'a self-styled poacher', explained his strange behaviour thus: 'I wanted to panic everybody. My intention was to scare the bloody daylights out of the governor.'

'Although,' he added, by way of mitigation, 'I have nothing against him, the staff, or the police.'

Another mitigating factor was that while Poddy had something of a reputation for eccentricity, he was not a man given to malice.

On one celebrated occasion he had nailed himself to a tree by the ear with a six-inch nail in a protest outside Stafford Crown Court, and appeared in court in a variety of bizarre outfits.

On another occasion he was charged – but later acquitted – of causing unnecessary suffering to a frog during an attempt on the world live frog swallowing record.

Before packing him off to spend six months as Her Majesty's – and Mr Pryor's – guest, the judge heard Mr Derek Halbert, defending, describe his client as 'a harmless, fun-loving character with a Walter Mitty mentality who is regarded with great affection in his locality.'

Bellyache

Unhappy burglar Eric Poole was even more relieved than his long-suffering public when he was jailed for five years.

His counsel told Exeter Crown Court: 'Freedom makes him nervous. He can't cope with life outside. He gets stomach cramp. It was a relief when he was caught.'

Poole, 53, has happily spent most of his adult life in prison – he has been sent there *fifty* times for some 400 offences.

Key role

Police called to a theatre in Barnstaple, Devon, where a play about Sherlock Holmes was being staged, were amused to find that the leading actor had locked himself in his own handcuffs. They spared the embarrassed thespian's blushes by freeing him from his dilemma minutes before curtain-up. The actor's name? William Chubb.

Life ban

'I warned him that if he came before me again for drunken driving he would regret it for the rest of his life,' Judge

Carmino Rioja told the court over which he was presiding in the Bolivian town of Potosi.

In the case of 28-year-old father-of-six Ramon Salinas that regret lasted for all of five minutes. That was how long it took court officials to carry out the Judge's sentence, which entailed dragging Salinas out into the street and executing him on the spot.

Judge Rioja's heavy-handed approach to the problem of drunk driving was blamed on the death of his five-year-old daughter Miranda, who a few months earlier had been crushed beneath the wheels of a truck driven by a drunk.

After his first appearance before the judge Salinas was packed off to serve a modest seven-day sentence. When he again appeared before him ten days later he wasn't so lucky.

'I was fair with him the first time, but he showed no respect for the law,' declared Judge Rioja, adding: 'I feel very sorry for his wife and children, though they are probably better off without him. But, now, he has respect for the law.

'Now my message is clear to everyone. Anyone convicted twice for drunken driving will be taken into the street and hanged where all the people can see it for themselves.

'There will be no time for appeal. I am the law, and my justice will be swift.'

News of Salinas's execution – reported in detail in one newspaper under the banner headline: 'Judge hands out stiff sentence' – not surprisingly triggered expressions of shock and outrage throughout the South American nation.

Declared one government official: 'The judge should be removed from the bench.

'The tragic death of his daughter has greatly affected his judgement. His overwhelming grief has been too much for him to bear.

'But he cannot be allowed to be judge and executioner in a city courtroom. He is to hear only minor traffic offences. These people aren't cold-blooded murderers.

'It is a national disgrace that a man – a young father with mouths to feed – is dragged into the street like a mad dog and hanged – for drunk driving!'

Rough justice, of course, works both ways, especially in South America, where violence is the order of the day. No one appeared unduly perturbed when the same government official declared: 'It's only a matter of time before someone in his courtroom pulls out a gun and puts a bullet in his head.'

In the cooler

A burglar kept his cool when police surrounded the pub he was raiding.

He dived into the deep freeze and hid there for 90 minutes until an officer casually lifted the lid and found him shivering inside.

Nottingham publican Jeff Sale said, 'He looked like Jack Frost. His face was deathly pale and his teeth were chattering.'

Pot luck

Thieves bound and gagged a young engineer before ransacking his Mayfair home. But when police arrived to free him they found marijuana growing in the flat, and arrested him instead.

In court, charged with growing cannabis, the man was given a conditional discharge after PC Nicholas Farmer told magistrates: 'Unfortunately the burglars were never caught. There is definitely an element of bad luck in this case.'

Auf Wiedersehn

Unable to make himself understood to the four Germans appearing before him, Sheriff Keith of Glasgow decided to postpone the trial until an interpreter could be found.

Raising his hand from the public benches Mr Robert Fife said that 'as an ex prisoner-of-war' he was prepared to translate. Proceeding, the Sheriff asked: 'What is your name?' Where upon Mr Fife turned to the defendants and barked: 'Vot iss your name, hein?' and was promptly arrested for contempt of court.

Innocents Abroad

One of the authors once reported a court hearing where a man charged with burglary asked the magistrate for bail on the grounds that he was innocent.

'You wouldn't be here if you were innocent,' snapped the beak. 'Bail refused.'

But it is a fact that the prison cells of Britain are busting at the seams with innocent men.

True, they were up to guilty business when they made the innocent mistake which landed them behind bars. But in this book, anyway, we judge them guilty of overwhelming innocence.

And lest legal minds take issue with us, it is worth remembering that the law, too, often makes an ass of itself. A perfectly innocent ass, of course.

Innocents Abroad

Keel-haul

Broke, jobless and generally down on his luck, one young man headed west to seek his fortune. The fact that he had absolutely no idea where on earth westward lay bothered him not at all.

Nor was his pioneering spirit dampened by his singular lack of sailing experience.

And so one night 19-year-old Eric Waite stole into Cardiff docks and chose himself a fine ocean-going yacht for his solo Atlantic crossing.

Waite was leaving nothing to chance. The Atlantic, he guessed, was about 500 miles across, and the passage would take three days. He stocked up for the trip with three packets of biscuits and a tin of baked beans.

At last the 33ft, £20,000 yacht, aptly named *Stowaway*, slipped anchor and eased out of the harbour bound for the open sea.

Or so the budding Chay Blyth thought.

Instead of turning right for New York, *Stowaway* turned left and headed up the Bristol Channel.

As the Eastern seaboard retreated even further into the distance, Waite, sensing something was wrong, opted to sail to Ireland instead. Some 20 miles later he was up the creek without a paddle when the yacht ran aground on its way to the River Severn. A rescue operation involving a helicopter, coastguards and a lifeboat was required to save him.

He later told the docks police: 'I tried to get a job in this country but there was no work. I decided to give America a try.'

Magistrate Sir Lincoln Hallinan, urging Waite to make things up with his parents, said: 'This is the only real way you will get back on an even keel.'

Asked outside the court if he would try again, Waite replied: 'No, it's too bloody dangerous by boat. Next time I'll try to steal a plane.'

Water-fall

Police are still fuming over the chance discovery by two Water Board employees in July 1984 of £5 million worth of irreplaceable silver heirlooms stolen from the Marquis of Tavistock's estate at Woburn Abbey.

The two men, on a routine inspection of a water switching station at Eaton Soton, Cambridgeshire, stumbled upon the booty just hours before the thieves were due to collect it. In so doing they wrecked a carefully planned police operation to catch the crooks redhanded and thus find the brains behind the multi-million pound robbery.

Double Take

Whereas most successful burglars will choose their haul with care and discretion, selecting only the best and most-easily-disposed-of goods, others have absolutely no taste whatsoever.

Like the thieves who broke into the Palace Theatre in Plymouth. They made off with 50 signed photographs of comedian Tom O'Connor – and then, clearly not satisfied with their haul, returned for more.

Still, could have been worse – could have been Des O'Connor.

Ransom, lose some

Some people are altogether too innocent for this life; like Tom King and his mate Dave Gill, for example. Their's is a touching story of innocence betrayed.

It started smoothly enough when they burst into Peter Smythe's flat and kidnapped him late one night.

The next stage was slightly trickier. They decided to ransom Mr Smythe back to himself. He did not appear to be unduly put out by this somewhat unusual practice.

The idea, his kidnappers explained, was that he should give all his money to them and they would give him back to himself. Trouble was, all his money was in the bank.

Undaunted, the kidnappers sat up all night guarding their victim in his own flat and waiting for the banks to open.

Came the dawn, they made Mr Smythe write out a cheque to empty his account. Then they escorted him down the road to his local branch.

It was at this point that things started to go slightly awry. Naturally the two men were reluctant to raise the cashier's suspicions, so they sent their victim inside to collect the ransom on himself.

Once free of his kidnappers, Mr Smythe seized his opportunity. He hastily scrawled on the back of the cheque: 'Call the police. Kidnapped.'

Meanwhile, outside, the enterprising kidnappers were doing their best to look inconspicuous as they waited for the ransom to be paid. They were still waiting hopefully when the police breezed up a few minutes later and arrested them.

Brought to book

The lonely passion of Sarah Brook could have been a tear-jerking novel; not that the lovelorn spinster would choose to read it.

Her passion was for books with happy endings, where strong and silent men clasped tremulous maidens to their breasts and swore undying love.

Miss Brook was in the act of clutching seven such books when she was arrested for shoplifting at Stoke-on-Trent.

It was then that the sad story of her own unrequited love began to unfold.

At her home detectives found another 483 stolen books, plundered over 13 years from the 22 branch libraries where she had worked.

They had titles like *The Secret Amour* and *The Runaway Heart*. Their pages were full of damsels in distress and clean-limbed heroes.

There were 41 long-playing records, too, and music cassettes of tender ballads.

'It is a case of what appears to be a lonely magpie,' the prosecution told the local court after the 32-year-old spinster admitted theft involving £2,563.

Afterwards a friend said: 'The romantic books were the wall she has built around herself. She reads 20 to 30 of the Mills and Boon sort every week. They give her what she cannot find in reality.'

A reality which, the court heard, did not include boyfriends.

'It is the saddest of cases. She has about 11 sisters and as one of the middle ones she feels she has somehow been forgotten,' said the friend by way of explanation.

Bureau de changeless

A robber found Canada's language barriers too much when he went into a Vancouver bank for French-speaking residents and handed a cashier a note in English demanding money. The cashier, a recent immigrant from China, was unable to read it, and called a colleague for assistance.

After puzzling over the note for several seconds the colleague asked the man to wait while he called the manager, who duly joined the fray. The man then mumbled something about 'money' in French, to which the bank manager replied: 'I'm sorry, but I don't speak English very well.'

In despair, the man asked for his note back, left the bank, and went into the English-speaking bank next door, where he started to go through the same procedure. This time he was more successful. The teller immediately handed over £500 in notes, and the raider, after thanking him in English, made off.

The invisible man

It wasn't at all like the movies when Bob Keaton stuck up a Brooklyn bank. No-one screamed, no-one panicked, no-one even tackled him.

Bob was playing his part all right. He shoved a demand note under the cashier's nose and, in the best B-movie fashion, growled: 'Give me all your money.'

Bank clerk Catherine Murphy looked him up and down and said: 'You've got to be kidding.'

'No, I'm not,' retorted the indignant bandit.

Mrs Murphy passed the note to the teller sitting next to her and remarked conversationally: 'Look what I've got.'

As an afterthought she pressed the alarm bell. The bank guard sauntered over and he, too, didn't think much of Bob's demand. Someone suggested maybe the assistant manager should have a look at the note. Bob, having been asked to wait, stepped back from the counter to let other customers be served.

While staff deliberated what to do about the hold-up, Bob stood nonchalantly leaning against a table, in perfect view of a security camera.

At length, bored with the poor service, he strolled out. While he was resting against a parking meter the police arrived and dashed straight past him into the bank.

'Hey!' he hollered after them, 'I'm the guy you want.'

Whereupon, as Judge Jack Weinstein summed up at the trial: 'The policeman thanked him for his help, and then arrested him.'

Fair dinkum, it's Burglar Bill

The envelope from Australia that dropped through the letter box of Mrs Brenda Gittins' home in Chaddesden, Derby, a month after it was broken into and the electricity meter raided, contained two $100 bills and a note which read:

'I'm the bloke what did your meter. I needed the money to get out here and help me start a new life. Now I'm doing great – but my conscience has been niggling me. So I enclose the money.'

The note was signed 'William Burglar'.

The money, equivalent to £130, replaced the stolen cash *and* gave Mrs Gittins a small bonus.

'I was terribly upset when the meter was broken into,' said Mrs Gittins after her unexpected windfall. 'Now I'm amazed – I can't stop laughing.'

Disarming evidence

Cross-examining a small boy whose right arm was alleged to have been crippled by the negligence of the omnibus company he was defending, F.E. Smith (later Lord Birkenhead) asked the lad to demonstrate to the court the extent of his terrible injuries.

'Will you show me just how high you can lift your arm,' said F.E.

The boy slowly brought his arm up to shoulder level, his face reflecting the pain it cost him to carry out the manoeuvre.

'Thank you,' said F.E. sympathetically. 'And now will you show me how high you could lift it before the accident.'

Immediately the lad shot his arm up above his head. Case dismissed.

Listen . . . but . . . I'm . . .!

Convicted of murder in 1863, Paul Hubert, from Bordeaux, languished in a French prison cell for 21 years despite daily protesting his innocence.

When someone finally got around to re-checking the charge sheet it was discovered that Hubert had been convicted of killing himself.

Birds of passage

There was something not quite shipshape – Bristols fashion – about the buxom girl on the cross-channel ferry.

It wasn't the way she wiggled when she walked that so entranced the matelots.

It was more the way she wiggled when she was standing still.

They were so moved by the spectacle they alerted Dover port authorities.

And on stepping ashore, the shapely passenger was asked to remove her sweater, whereupon a sparrow fluttered free from her bosom.

The bird was her pet and she was taking it on holiday, the girl explained. But she still ran foul of quarantine laws, and her sparrow had to be put down.

Frosty reception

There was one flaw in Ian Bishop's big burglary plan, but he couldn't find it. He couldn't find the house, either, so he had to stop people, asking them for directions.

And because the house in question was the country retreat of top TV personality David Frost at Leiston, Suffolk, they took particular notice of him.

As his counsel told Ipswich Crown Court, where Bishop was sentenced to three and a half years, 'Only the most idiotic burglar would go around asking for directions.'

Besides, counsel added, market trader Bishop 'could hardly have passed as one of Mr Frost's weekend guests.'

Artless

Thieves at St Clement's hospital in East London may not have known much about art, but they knew what they liked. Which possibly explains why they made off with frozen chicken legs and a few large tins of coffee, scorning paintings worth £1,000.

A hospital spokesman said, 'Obviously they had a good

look at the paintings because they were knocked about a bit. They mustn't have liked them.'

Art dekko

Then there were the artless robbers who burst into Mrs Moira Millen's house, tied her up, and demanded, 'Where is your valuable painting?'

The terrified housewife obediently pointed out L. S. Lowry's *Dockside, Sunderland, 1962*, a work worth some £20,000.

It was a typical Lowry scene, a smokey Northern backdrop peopled with those famous matchstick men and matchstick cats and dogs.

But the two thieves, a pair of Philistines if ever there was, thought it a load of old junk.

'They said it couldn't be worth anything and threw it on the floor,' said Mrs Millen, barely concealing her disgust.

'I was too frightened to lie, and eventually they believed me and made off with it.'

They also made off with her Aston Martin – but only after asking her: 'How do you release the handbrake?'

Short and curlies

Carrot-topped Dean Saunders dyed his flaming locks jet black to escape detection after a knifepoint robbery. Pity he forgot about his ginger moustache.

I've bin a wild rover

Back at the station, it must have taken some explaining . . .

But as the embarrassed sergeant probably recorded the incident: 'I was proceeding in an orderly fashion in my police patrol Rover adjacent to the village of Staxton, North Yorkshire, when I observed a car which I had reason to believe was stolen.

'I indicated the driver to stop and when the vehicle had

come to a standstill, I approached him. I found him to be a man of around six-foot in height, slim-built and of a rough appearance.

'He was clad in a plastic dustbin liner.

'When I endeavoured to question the man, he leapt from the vehicle, pushed me aside, jumped into my patrol car and drove off at some considerable speed.

'I then noticed that he had also removed the keys from the vehicle he had been driving. However, I sought assistance from a passing motorist and we pursued the man at speeds of up to 100 mph. We were unable to apprehend him.

'The police car was later found abandoned in a ditch 10 miles from the scene of the incident.'

Local people duly reported seeing 'a wild-eyed dishevelled

man' escaping with a bad limp and a rather creased bin liner.

Police warned the man could be dangerous and should not be approached. They also advised their officers not to be so daft as to leave their keys in the ignition in future.

Crime wave

Maybe it sounds a bit like the act of the Good Samaritan crossing the road to help the out-of-luck thief pinch his neighbour's ass, but that's the way these things happen.

It was down at Shaldon in Devon and these three villains were trying to nick an 18 ft speedboat called Mahlady.

But on account of the tide being out, and so forth, they couldn't get it up the sand. At this juncture the Good Samaritan, in the shape of several sunbathers, lent a hand.

They, too, strained but it was still no use. So the thieves then used a Land Rover, also stolen, to tow it to the main road.

Some 50 cheering holidaymakers held up traffic to let them get away.

As rueful boatowner Eddie Hand commented: 'The sheer cheek of the devils is unbelievable.'

Thank slot

An Old Bailey judge allowed armed robber Raymond Hill to stay at home during his trial to recover from 'flu. The 'flu flew and so did Hill.

In another case, the same Judge Peter Slot let an alleged burglar leave the dock to feed his parking meter. He didn't come back either.

Conviction addiction

Enumerable Vaillant and Jose Moreno made their first mistake of the night when they broke into a house in search of drugs and began terrorising the elderly couple who lived there, and two of their friends.

For the house singled out for their raid, in a suburb of Miami, was the wrong one. The place they were looking for – a known haunt of drug addicts and pushers – was next door.

Once inside the mistakes began to snowball.

First they cut the coiled cord from an electric can opener, thinking it was the telephone line. Then, when one of the robbers pulled a gun on the elderly couple, the bullets fell out.

And the only drugs they found were a handful of nytroglycerine pills the old man was taking for a heart condition.

In despair the bumbling burglars fled the house with their pitiful haul – a small amount of cash, the old man's heart pills, a few bottles of booze, and the woman's diamond ring, which they managed to drop in the street in their rush to get away.

The climax of the caper came when the driver of the getaway car sped past the guard house at the entrance to the Homestead United States Air Force Base after mistaking it for a toll booth on the nearby turnpike. Military police had little difficulty rounding up the gang and placing them under close arrest.

The last act in their comedy of errors played to a full house before Judge Michael Salmon in the Miami Circuit Court in 1985 where the pair were convicted of armed robbery, theft, burglary and false imprisonment.

Elementary, my dear Watson

As Holmes once remarked to his trusty aide, 'Crime is common. Logic is rare. Therefore it is upon the logic rather than the crime that you should dwell.' Of course, you don't necessarily need a Sherlock Holmes to bring a blunderer to book. . . .

Elementary, my dear Watson

Heavy-handed

After an increase was noted in the number of reports involving robberies at luxurious villas and apartments in the Egyptian town of Giza, senior police officers decided to intensify surveillance in the area and commissioned a special squad for the purpose.

Despite offering a £20,000 reward, efforts to bring the villains to book proved embarrassingly unsuccessful.

When they finally apprehended Wafig Fayed, a 28-year-old car mechanic, and charged him with stealing £1 million worth of goods over a three-month period, deputy prime minister Nabawi Ismail explained the delay thus: 'This highly-successful thief had managed to avoid detection because he had six fingers on this hand, thus confusing the fingerprint department of the Giza police'.

Wrongfooted

Teenage burglar Patrick Lukeman was pleased to note that actor Nigel Havers took the same size in footwear as he.

He also approved of the other man's taste. So much so that halfway through a raid on the actor's London home, Lukeman kicked off his old shoes in favour of a pair he found in the bedroom.

When his own pair were duly discovered, under the bed, detectives were heartened to note they clearly bore the thief's name inside.

The 17-year-old raider, who with partner Kenneth Ross netted £500 in jewellery and property from the actor, got three months in a detention centre.

43

Family allowance

Asked by magistrate Mr Dudley Reynolds why he stole 757 sweaters, 733 men's shirts, 460 dresses, 403 jackets, 83 pairs of socks and 286 pairs of children's trousers, worth in all about £14,000, Mr Taruvingia Homwe, a 37-year-old resident of Harare, Zimbabwe, explained, 'I have a large family.'

Telly-ad

The new TV programme was one of those brilliant ideas that was destined to run and run, as the showbiz people say.

For the firm of Milan auctioneers reasoned that with a captive afternoon audience of women sitting at home with a few hours to spare, selling jewellery should be a cinch.

So much for the idea. But there were a few details in the execution of it that didn't work out quite right, as they discovered shortly after they went on the air when police burst in and seized cases of stolen jewels, paintings and ivory ornaments – the spoils from a string of robberies.

It transpired that one of their 'customers', a Milan housewife who had been sitting at home toying with the remote control of her TV set, had chanced upon the programme just as a bracelet, a gift from her husband, was in the process of being auctioned off to telephone bidders.

When the next lot, her ring, appeared on the screen, she phoned in with the top bid of £770 – and then promptly called the police.

Curses!

Stumbling around an office in the dark, a Cardiff burglar kept bumping himself on pieces of furniture. Next day police had the bemused and bruised man under arrest. In his blundering progress around the office he had knocked over a dictating machine which switched itself on . . . and recorded his every movement. Detectives were able to recognise his voice from his muffled oaths.

Booked

Jilted bookie Denis Poole thought he was on to a winner when he launched a porno-picture blackmail campaign against his beautiful blonde ex-mistress.

The odds, however, were somewhat stacked against him. Police had little difficulty in tracking down the blackmailing betting shop boss after identifying the man in one of the compromising photographs as none other than Poole himself.

After hearing that Poole had sent photographs of himself and the woman together to her husband – one of them stuck inside a Christmas card; plastered the husband's car windscreen with other compromising photographs; and had sent still more lurid pictures to friends and neighbours in the Cumbria village where they lived; Judge Alistair Bell branded him 'an old-fashioned blackguard', and sent him to jail for eighteen months.

Elementary, my dear Watson

Sherlock Holmes would have spotted the elementary blunder. Mark Holmes did not.

Which is why, less than an hour after his fouled-up hold-up, detectives ran the hapless Holmes to ground.

In his raid on a Harrogate, Yorkshire, off-licence he had presented the owner with a note demanding cash. It also contained Holmes' name. And his address. And even his postcode.

Shopkeeper John Patterson burst out laughing when he read it. Still chuckling, he made Holmes step aside while he served another customer.

Then, armed only with a bottle of Coke, he chased Holmes off before handing police the note.

The art of coarse fishing

He was an average specimen, the one who nearly got away. He looked just like any other man among the shoals of holiday anglers who haunt the waters of California's Lake Vail Fishing Camp.

He breezed up in a car loaded to the gun'wales with rods, waders, reels and flies. Like everyone else, Stephen Migdal rented a boat, and off he chugged.

But there was one thing missing from Migdal's equipment which rather bothered camp manager Roger Wiberg, an ex-policeman.

And because of it he kept a close watch on his fishy customer. Sure enough, that very night, he saw Migdal hoist a heavy sack from his car boot, ferry it out to the centre of the lake and silently dump it in the water.

Police were called and the sack, containing a woman's body, recovered. Migdal owned up. She was his wife, and he had murdered her.

And how did the camp manager catch on that he was up to no good? Simple, really. Migdal had forgotten to buy a four-dollar fishing permit.

Stoolpigeon

In a string of 30 burglaries a teenage Texan gang netted half-a-million pounds. Then somebody squawked on them.

Well, some*thing*, actually; a parrot called Baby.

Three days after his owners' Baytown home was looted of £10,000 in cash and jewellery, Baby started gabbing, 'Come here Robbie, come here Ronnie.'

This bewildered Baby's owners, Mike and Tobye Madison. They had no friends called Ronnie or Robbie, so they told detectives.

Within hours gangleader Robert Davis and two of his henchmen were behind bars.

Come here, Baby,

Sketchy details

Police didn't need one of those vague identikit descriptions to catch the man who raped a young art student.

They had his own 'commissioned' portrait to go by.

Before brutally assaulting his victim he ordered her to draw him. Her unfinished sketch helped police identify Lester Nelson, who at the Old Bailey was jailed for three-and-a-half years.

Paddy-stani

Brendan Moloney's accent was a dead giveaway. Especially as the social security cheque he was trying to cash was clearly made out to one Abdul Khaliq.

Undeterred, Moloney flourished his Irish birth certificate when an assistant at the Birmingham welfare office asked for proof of his identity.

Although the 47-year-old Irishman had taken the trouble to cross out his name and write in the name 'Abdul Khaliq' in its place, staff remained unimpressed, and Moloney was arrested, charged and duly fined £100 for deception.

The Wrong Arm of the Law

The law is a ass, a idiot, quoth Mr Bumble. Experience
has shown that the people who administer it are often
sadly lacking too. . . .

The Wrong Arm of the Law

Déjà vu

During the course of a case he was hearing from the bench Mr Justice Avory (1851-1935) asked a witness whether he had ever been convicted of a criminal offence. The witness agreed that he had, but explained that his conviction was 'due to the incapacity of my counsel rather than to any fault on my part.'

'It always is, and you have my sincere sympathy,' said the judge with a smile.

'And I deserve it,' replied the witness, 'seeing as you were my counsel on that occasion.'

Bar brawl

After watching a ball game at Arlington, Texas, 40 members of the Dallas County Criminal Bar Association ordered their coach drivers to stop, alighted, and began brawling among themselves.

The incident was recounted afterwards by a bemused Dallas police sergeant, Steve Morrow, who said, 'I was amazed to see upwards of 50 defence attorneys, county prosecutors, judges and senior investigators, gouging and kicking each other along the freeway. When I tried to stop them I was told that they were lawyers and knew what they were doing, and that if I didn't beat it I would be charged with harassment. The following day I visited the District Attorney's office where I was told that nothing of the kind had occurred.'

Whisky galore

For the two boating friends off for a weekend jolly on their motor cruiser *Papyrus*, the homeward run from Guernsey promised to be the most enjoyable – and certainly the most rewarding – part of the whole trip.

Stashed away below deck were 125 litres of whisky and wine and 9,000 cigarettes, all bought duty free and being shipped home in such a manner as to avoid the unnecessary expense and inconvenience of having to declare the haul to those rotten old customs and excise people, who somehow manage to take all the enjoyment out of smoking and drinking and life's other little pleasures.

They hadn't reckoned, however, on the unlikely event of something going wrong, although when the *Papyrus* developed engine trouble off Ramsgate and had to be towed into harbour by a customs boat the two men were still not unduly worried. After all, was not their illicit haul well hidden from prying eyes. And who, in any event, would suspect a High Court Judge of smuggling?

For the customs men involved, the discovery of the smugglers' hoard and the arrest of circuit court judge Keith Bruce Campbell and his associate, second-hand car dealer Alan Foreman, was something of a coup.

It was also an event that would be remembered in years to come as much for what the judge and his accomplice said about the crime, as for the crime itself.

Publican John Cheesman, whose Queens Head pub is bang opposite the Customs House to which the two men were taken after their arrest, recounts how he took ale with the shamefaced judge later that same evening. Challenged about his strange behaviour, the judge replied, in his best villains' vernacular, 'It was a fair cop, guv. They got us banged to rights.'

Mr Foreman, who was co-owner of the *Papyrus* and an old friend of the judge, summed up the incident in similar terms when the two subsequently appeared in court in Ramsgate: 'We went for a fishing trip and got some fags and booze. It's a fair cop.'

Before being found guilty of smuggling and fined £2,000 the judge told the magistrate by way of explanation: 'You know our way of life. I'm afraid we drink half-a-dozen bottles over a weekend.'

It was a way of life that was to come to an abrupt end five days later when the Lord Chancellor, Lord Hailsham dismissed Judge Bruce Campbell from his £29,750-a-year job, thus bestowing upon him the dubious distinction of being the first judge in modern times to be sacked for a criminal offence.

Master of deception

Of course, Bruce Campbell – described somewhat uncharitably by Fleet Street columnist Jean Rook as 'a grasping old fool' who 'paid for (his folly) with his career and his reputation' – was not the first eminent member of the judiciary to fall from grace in so ignominious a fashion.

John Parker, Earl of Macclesfield, friend and confidant of Walpole, Lord Lieutenant of Oxfordshire and Warwickshire, recognised as a great equity judge, until recently Lord Chief Justice and now, in 1725, Lord Chancellor, was caught with his fingers in the Chancery till and impeached by Parliament.

He was found guilty of fraud and deception (he had, in fact

been party to a racket which involved selling Masterships in Chancery at 5,000 guineas a throw), dismissed, disgraced, fined £30,000 – a handsome sum in those days – and imprisoned in the Tower for six weeks until the money to pay the fine had been raised.

He retired to a small house near Derby, where he languished for seven years until his death at the age of 66, in 1732 – as historian Anthony Mockler put it, 'yet another hopelessly corrupt judge, as so many of our Lord Chief Justices have been.'

The lad was described as lazy, and when his mother asked him to go to work he threatened to smash her brains out. The case was adjourned for three weeks to give the lad another chance. – **From a Manchester newspaper**

False alarm

Called out by the police in the wee small hours to switch off his shop's burglar alarm, Roger Gravelling drove to the scene dressed only in a nightshirt and slippers. He was promptly breathalysed, and charged with driving over the limit.

But magistrates at Cambridge gave him an absolute discharge because he had been answering a police emergency call. Said Mr Gravelling relievedly, 'I am delighted and over the moon.'

Long arm of the law

Despite a 10-year sentence for plotting the murder of two political rivals, Sheriff Paul Browning managed to keep his star.

He ran his Harlan County office by long distance telephone from inside a maximum security prison in Kentucky.

Vietnam veteran Browning, 38, was eventually forced to quit office after a Federal judge complained that he was neglecting his duties.

* * *

The good folks in Dawson County, way down in deepest Georgia, took a more charitable view of their sheriff's little peccadilloes.

Despite doing a spell in the penitentiary for running moonshine, they re-elected John Davis to his third term of office.

When last heard of he was back in the slammer again . . . for drug trafficking.

Oh! Sullivan

Sentencing a swindler to a lenient two year stretch, the judge told him: 'I am quite prepared to accept that you are a perfectly decent person . . . apart from these matters.'

'These matters' referred to Michael O'Sullivan's 10 year career of crime, during which time he committed 632 offences – one every 5.7 days on average.

O'Sullivan owned up to 37 burglaries and 595 frauds involving a grand total of £9,000, most of which he spent on booze.

But Judge Martin at the Old Bailey heard that O'Sullivan hated violence, and was always the perfect gentleman.

He specialised in stealing cheques and forging the owner's signatures. When he was caught trying to pass one in a West End bank in London he immediately confessed to the other 631 offences, even though police had not connected him with them.

The rapists' friend

Old Bailey judge Michael Argyle QC is no stranger to controversy either.

In June 1982 he earned himself the dubious title 'the rapists' friend' after acquitting a Hell's Angel up on a rape charge.

He was back in the headlines again a year later after hearing the case against a man who tore the clothes off a top model, tried to rape her, banged her head on the floor, slapped her about the face, and then grabbed her round the throat.

On that occasion he told the man, barman Malcolm Rock

'You come from Derby, which is my part of the world. Now off you go and don't come back to this court.'

Not surprisingly his remarks incurred the wrath of the anti-rape brigade, the whole of Fleet Street, and a sizeable chunk of the public at large. His standing was not helped much when, in setting Rock free, he told him, 'For goodness sake make this the last time.

'Once you put your hands around a woman's neck when you are in drink anything can happen.'

His decision to suspend Rock's jail sentence for two years was due in part to the fact that Rock was said to have become remorseful after the attack, and had offered to send flowers to his victim.

It was that judgement, and the remarks that preceded it, that prompted the *Daily Express* to comment:-

'That remark turned everybody's part of an insecure and terrifying world upside down. It's the old boys' network riddled with frightening loopholes, when a judge slaps his fellow countryman on the wrist, if not on the back, and all but playfully tells him to run away but don't get involved in that game again.

'Recent suspect judgement has stirred the dust. The biggest wigs must now be thoroughly examined.

'Because if you can't trust even a judge we are all lost in the lawless jungle. With our belief in British justice battered and brutally raped.'

Merry Christmas

Meanwhile, Judge Lord Patrick Dunboyne was giving two young thugs in his court a similarly bizarre admonishing.

After admitting being involved in a burglary in which a 15-year-old girl was punched unconscious, the teenage pair were told by the judge, 'You should be thoroughly ashamed of yourselves.'

Then, with the judge's best wishes ringing in their ears, they were led away to spend three weeks in a detention centre.

'I hope you get this over with before the holiday,' Judge Duboyne told them. 'And I hope you have a happy Christmas.'

The girl's incredulous mother said after the verdict, 'How could a judge say such a thing?'

Smørgas-bored

In Sweden, whenever they get bored, they make up a new law about something. And as Sweden isn't the most exciting of God's countries, they have an awful lot of pretty weird laws.

Take the case of shoplifter Ulla Pearson. Police reckoned they had her banged to rights stealing sweaters from a store.

In her house they found 90 stolen dresses waiting to be sold, and £73,000 – her proceeds from ten years of shoplifting. They seized the lot.

Ulla, 30, went to jail for a year, during which time psychiatrists figured out she was a kleptomaniac. She emerged cured, but somewhat aggrieved.

She brightened up, however, on learning that under one of those quaint Swedish laws she was due a £65,000 refund from the State.

It seems that a shoplifter is entitled to hold on to the value of all the unclaimed goods. And just as a bonus Ulla was also due a year's interest at eight percent.

As State bailiff Ramon Berger observed, 'It is remarkable that she should get this money back. It seems there is a loophole in our legal system.'

But all is not lost. Swedish Inland Revenue officials apparently while away their boredom by dreaming up new tax laws. At the time of going to press they were working on Ulla's case.

Said one, 'We are still working out how much is owed. Perhaps we can stop her plans to retire after all.'

Pet hate

Hauled before a Libyan People's Court charged with biting a man, the prisoner said not a word in his defence.

He just wagged his tail.

Despite which the prisoner, a dog, was jailed for a month on a strict diet of bread and water.

With a terrible twanging and banging, plinking and plonking, the prisoner was led into court.

Around his neck hung a guitar which made itself heard with every move he made.

But it wasn't just that which so offended magistrate Derek Fairclough. There was also the fellow's clothes sense.

He was wearing, reading from the top down . . . a floppy black beret, a denim jerkin, and luminous green briefs. No trousers, you'll note.

Mr Fairclough noticed this too. He promptly ordered the man to dump the hat and the guitar and get himself a pair of trousers. Pronto.

Well, the first two bits were easy, but where on earth was he to find the pants in a hurry?

The prisoner's solicitor, Barry Cuttle, and his clerk, Michael Tracey, frantically canvassed the court building.

Strangely, they couldn't find a soul willing to lend them his trousers. Mr Cuttle was desperate.

And then he began to look thoughtfully at the fetching brown tweeds his clerk was wearing. Oh no, thought the unhappy Mr Tracey.

'It's only for a few minutes,' Mr Cuttle coaxed. 'We'll have him out on bail in no time.'

Mr Tracey gave in. He hid himself in a small room and handed over the tweeds.

A minute later the now guitar-less, beret-less prisoner was back in the dock, and the trousers suited him down to the ground.

Mr Cuttle rose to defend him on theft charges and, as confidently predicted, the hearing lasted only a few minutes.

But the gallant solicitor had got one thing wrong. The prisoner was remanded in custody.

And a speechless Mr Cuttle stood by helplessly as his client, together with his clerk's trousers, exited en route to Manchester's Strangeways prison.

A girl assistant dashed off to the custody office to have the man debagged. But no one there believed a word of her story.

Ho, ho, ho, said the laughing policeman. 'Someone's pulling your leg.'

Meanwhile, Mr Tracey was still in his underpants in his little room and getting somewhat anxious. He thought he had been forgotten, but was too embarrassed to go out and remind someone.

At last, just as the brown tweeds were vanishing into a black maria, a court official recovered them.

Back in his own trousers again, Mr Tracey said: 'I'll never live this down.'

This is a particularly serious offence which we have to deal with severely as a detergent to anyone in the same mind. – **From the** *Leicester Mercury*

A load of Bullingham

Charged with murder in 1812, John Bullingham protested that he had never intended to assassinate the Chancellor of the Exchequer and the First Lord of the Treasury, Sir Spencer Perceval, and that the shot which killed him as he entered the lobby of the House of Commons was in fact meant for Lord Leveson Gower, a former ambassador to Russia.

Calculated arrest

To err, as they say, is human – so there's absolutely no excuse for the FBI computer which caused 17,340 people to be arrested on the same day. It had wrongly listed them as wanted criminals.

Dog-gone

Hot on the heels of a runaway robber, Boss, a four-year-old tracker dog, carried on the chase alone after his handler fell and hurt himself.

The crook was soon caught but Boss vanished. Embarrassed police at Helsingborg, Sweden, had to appeal to the public to help find their lost alsatian.

Holy deliverance

John Popham, the one-time mugger and highwayman who went on to become Elizabeth I's Lord Chief Justice, was not the only eminent personage who indulged in a bit of spare-time criminal activity to bolster his income.

In 1850, Bishop Raphoe, another enthusiastic part-time highwayman, was shot and killed by one of his intended victims while carrying out a robbery on Hounslow Heath.

Although the story was covered up to save the Church unnecessary embarrassment, a cryptic reference in the *Gentleman's Magazine* told of the Bishop's being taken mysteriously ill on Hounslow Heath, and dying of 'an inflammation of the bowels.'

Bad form

On the eve of a visit by two community police officers to a Hampshire comprehensive school, the headmaster briefed his teachers: 'Two members of the staff must be present to preserve order.'

Dutch treat

Police chief Bernard Malipaard was anxious to discover the stuff potential girl recruits were made of.

He told pretty candidates: 'Show me your breasts – or let me unbutton your blouse.'

Bernard was sacked from his job in Zwijndrecht, Holland, after one girl complained about his unorthodox screening.

Accused of abusing his powers, he vainly protested he just wanted to test the girls' character.

'The aim was that they should say no,' he explained.

The Wages of Sin

The wages of sin is death; so saith the Good Book
(Romans, 6.22). Well, perhaps that was the going rate
back in the old days of an eye for an eye and so forth, but
nowadays the payout is rather less niggardly. In this
enlightened age, the worst that sinners might expect is a
life sentence. Well, maybe not *quite* the worst. For there
is indeed a fate worse than life . . . humiliation.

The Wages of Sin

Small potatoes

As staff in a chip shop counted the day's takings, they were confronted by a hooded man wielding a knife.

He ordered the manageress, 'Fish and chips twice, pie and chips once.'

He coolly insisted on having them salted, vinegared and wrapped before vanishing into the night with his 89p haul.

John Thompson, owner of the Manchester chip shop, said: 'The till was full of cash. In all my 25 years in the business I have never known anything so daft. I know potatoes are expensive, but this is ridiculous.

. 'I only wonder why he didn't go the whole hog and ask for peas as well.'

Knick-knack nick nicked

A woman shoplifter picked the wrong target when she tried to steal from a charity sale.

For the sale was being held inside a top security prison – and the stalls were all manned by convicted killers.

The nicker in the nick was among 200 guests visiting London's Wormwood Scrubs jail for a public performance of a play staged by the prisoners, followed by a sale in aid of charity of stuffed toys, leatherware and other knick-knacks made in the prison workshop.

She was let off with a stern warning from a 'lifer' who told her, 'Crime doesn't pay, lady. If it did, we wouldn't be here.'

Open and shut case

Before they laid their thieving mitts on it, the safe at the leisure centre was a pretty secure affair.

But after the gang had done with it, it was, well, er, . . . as safe as houses.

Instead of cutting it open they welded it shut. It took staff an hour to hammer and chisel it open again to find its contents untouched.

Said a Chichester, Sussex, detective, 'The thieves must have been complete amateurs.'

There was only £150 in the safe anyway.

Gang bang

Despite a legend to the contrary, Jesse James and his gang will go down in history as probably the most incompetent band of robbers the Wild West had ever seen.

In 1876 Jesse and the other members of the James-Youger gang hit the First National Bank in Northfield, Minnesota. In the ensuing gunfight, which involved passers-by as well as bank staff, guards, lawmen and the gang themselves, two men were shot dead and another five wounded.

As the smoke of battle cleared away the gang staggered off and headed for the hills with their haul. This was later discovered to total just $12, which worked out at $1.71c for every man shot.

Cheeky lot

The lorry hi-jack at Valentigny, Northern France, turned out to be a real bum job. Only half an hour after it was stolen, the truck was found abandoned, complete with its cargo of . . . 180,000 babies' nappies.

Diamonds aren't forever

It should have been a gem of a job, but bungling burglar Edwin Juett blew it wide open.

With three masked confederates he tied up Mrs Joan Thomas in the living room of her home in Datchet, Buckinghamshire, and proceeded to blow open the safe with gelignite.

Trouble was they used so much that when the dust settled

there was nothing left of the small fortune in diamonds they had come to collect save for a few worthless splinters.

Even more frustrating was when he got caught and sent to jail for seven years.

Tea break-in

Having successfully raided an engineering works to steal heavy flame cutting equipment, thieves at Yate, Bristol, then spent hours using it to cut through a heavy steel safe in another factory.

When they finally burned their way through, the gang found a large packet of PG Tips tea, sugar and a jar of coffee.

Police described the man they were seeking as 'disappointed'.

In a raid on Partington Railway Station during the weekend, thieves stole four dozen pencils and three dozen ball-point pen refills.

They told The Guardian *that their headmaster was very pleased with their success and the honour it reflected on the school.*
– From the *Sale and Stratford Guardian*

Poor excuse

The wages of sin ain't all they're cracked up to be, as the High Holborn gang admitted.

Fleeing, empty-handed, after a cock-eyed hold-up, one shouted to City office staff, 'Sorry about this, but it's our living.'

Office manager Alan Lynch said, 'The way they were jumping about when they came in, we thought it was a joke. Then we saw that they had shotguns and knives.

'I told them the keys of the safe weren't here, although the clerk who had them was sitting just behind me.'

The gang tried to blast open the safe holding £5,000, but only succeeded in breaking a window.

Costly undertaking

Undertaker Michael Bachelor hit on a safe hiding place for the £1,250 cash he stole from his employers – he hid it in a coffin.

But the coffin, along with the booty inside it, was cremated before Bachelor had a chance to retrieve his illicit haul.

'I tucked it into the shroud on an old man's chest,' he told a court in Kingston, Surrey, after explaining, 'A coffin in a chapel of rest is the last place anyone would think of looking. People are loath to go there'.

'Unfortunately,' he added, 'I didn't remember the money until it was too late.'

Bachelor's carelessness did not end there. The court also heard that of the £4,600 he had already been convicted of stealing, he somehow managed to leave another £1,500 of it on a bus.

* * *

John Deering also thought he'd found the perfect hiding place for the £700 he'd stolen from the firm of undertakers he worked for.

Like Mr Bachelor he, too, hid the money in a coffin for safekeeping. And just like Mr Bachelor before him, he also forgot to take it out until it was too late, with the result that by the time he'd remembered, the coffin, the cash and the body had all gone to that Great Accounting House in the sky.

Explaining that Mr Deering had hidden the money in one of 20 coffins available to him at the time, defence counsel Mr Ronald Trot said, 'The £700 was Mr Deering's responsibility and he didn't want to risk taking it home with him. The office did not have a safe, so he left it in a full coffin. It's the sort of place people just don't look.'

Even after Mr Deering had been convicted on 16 counts of

theft and false accounting, and given a nine months' suspended jail sentence, the mystery over the fate of the money remained unsolved.

'It's not known whether it was buried or cremated,' the court at Snaresbrook, East London, was told.

Interviewed outside the court, Mr Deering said, 'I don't want to discuss the reason why I put the money in the coffin. It's gone. I don't know where it is, and I just want to forget about the whole thing.'

Doing bird

Thieves who stole a rare Mynah bird from a pet shop in Witham, Essex, were in for a shock. Said its owner: 'It does a perfect imitation of a police car siren.'

A fine mess

If only Cowsley Nowell had not tried so hard to be a law-abiding citizen he might not have turned out such a crook.

There was the time he was late in reporting to the police station over some previous offence. So he 'borrowed' a car to get there. But en route it was spotted by a police patrol car, which gave chase. Nowell panicked, crashed, and ended up in even more trouble.

The next problem was he couldn't afford to pay his fines because he was out of work. Rather than get into more bother with the law, Nowell took to the streets with an imitation gun to raise the money.

At the Old Bailey, Judge Underhill erred, if anything, in understatement when he described Nowell's subsequent life of crime as 'amateurish in the extreme'.

The first attempted robbery, at an off-licence, failed when someone hurled a beer can at him. Three days later he had to flee again after a shop assistant threatened him with an iron bar.

But it was third time lucky when Nowell held up a Dagenham fish 'n' chip shop. He made off with the entire contents of the till . . . £1.

Ten minutes later he was at it again, this time trying to stage a hold-up at a house. The angry owner came out, socked him one, and Nowell ran off empty-handed.

Four days after that came the big job, a raid on a Walthamstow newsagent's, which netted him £10. But he was soon spotted by police and arrested.

After all that, Nowell was given a two-year suspended sentence – and he still hadn't paid those fines.

Quids pro quo

The man who broke into newsagent John Walmsley's home had to write the night off as a total loss.

He was caught red-handed when Mr Walmsley unexpectedly returned to the house at Bridlington, Yorkshire.

There followed a 10-minute tussle. Breaking free, the burglar thrust £23 into his victim's hand 'to pay for the damage', and fled.

Said Mr Walmsley, 'I must be the only man in Britain to make a profit out of being burgled.'

Hell's grannies

There are certain mythological creatures one hears a lot about. There's Santa Claus, and the Easter Bunny, and the Tooth Fairy.

And then there's the frail little old lady, or FLOL.

The annals of crime are littered with tales of disillusioned villains who thought they had found a soft target in a FLOL.

More often than not the villain ends up the victim, having been punched, scratched, gouged, battered and kicked black and blue by some silver-haired old age pensioner armed with nothing more than a walking-stick.

Or, if they are in charitable mood, the FLOLs treat the baddies like ill-mannered children. Such was the fate of two armed youngsters who tried to raid a Kingston-upon-Thames, Surrey, Post Office.

For some lunatic reason they chose to do it on pension day. When they tried to force their way to the counter, the old girls shoved them right to the back of the queue again.

Somewhat incensed by this treatment, one raider waved his gun in the air and shouted all manner of threats. No one took a blind bit of notice.

So he marched up to an empty counter and laid the pistol on the parcel scales.

Model Nikki Critcher reported she was horrified to see the scales turn almost three-quarters of the way round.

'Next thing I knew was that someone had pressed the panic button, one of the cashiers was in tears, and the place was full of police.'

The senior citizens collected their pensions and went home as if nothing had happened.

Press-gang

Mind you, 75-year-old Mrs Evelyn Freestone had the power of the press behind her.

Armed with a rolled-up newspaper, the tiny widow routed a 6-ft tall knifeman *and* his mate from her village store in Great Cornard, Suffolk.

Said she: 'There was no way I was going to give in.'

Bomb surprise

And then there was the pair of West Country burglars who were reported to be shell-shocked after tangling with 71-year-old Mrs Jane Butler.

The two men, armed with clubs, fled when she grabbed an empty mortar shell, an ornament in her caravan home near Bath, and battered them around the head with it.

Police later caught up with the men when they sought hospital treatment . . . one for severe bruises, the other for a broken neck bone.

Out of the frying pan . . .

In a similarly bruising encounter a Bournemouth burglar was lucky to escape with his life and his trousers.

Finding him crouched in her toilet in the wee small hours, pensioner Bessy Mertens reached for the frying pan and gave him a rare old battering.

In his struggle to escape he lost a shoe, both socks, and ripped the hem of his trousers.

All Bessy, 64, lost was her best frying pan. 'I bent it so badly on the man I won't be able to use it again,' she said, adding with a grin of satisfaction, 'I wanted to bash the living daylights out of him.'

Later a slightly-bashed man with a badly bruised ego was helping with police enquiries.

Hoodwinked

'I wish he had broken his neck,' declared 72-year-old Miss Violet Scott, after she and her sister, Gladys, 69, had chased off an armed raider.

The man, over 6-ft tall, heavily hooded and wielding a club, tumbled down two flights of steps as the sisters hustled him out of their Plymouth corner shop.

Said Gladys: 'He couldn't see where he was going in that hood.'

Paper wait

Armed raiders staged a carefully-planned lorry hijack at Lenham, Kent. It was loaded with toilet rolls. Despite their reactions on seeing the haul, the raiders fled empty-handed.

Collared

Crime certainly didn't pay for Douglas Sykes. His dreams of ill-gotten riches netted a haul of just 26p and two shirts in eight successive raids.

So unsuccessful was he at his illicit trade that when, on his ninth and least successful sortie, he climbed through an

anonymous-looking window in Gateshead, County Durham, he found himself in the ladies loo of a bank by mistake.

By the time he realised his error alarm bells had already started to ring in the nearby police station. When a policeman and the bank manager arrived on the scene they discovered Sykes cowering under a typist's desk.

As he was led away Sykes blurted out, 'I didn't know it was a bank until I saw the big safe.'

In court Sykes' solicitor explained 'One's reaction here is to say, "We have got a bank robber". Nothing could be further from the truth.

'He was entirely unaware that he was in a bank. As a thief he was a miserable failure.'

Taking the piss

And just in passing, the raider who snatched a bank bag from a doctor's assistant in Johannesburg, South Africa, was more than somewhat disappointed to find that it contained just 10 bottles of human urine.

Don't Move, *this is a cock-up*

The bungling bank robber who held the shotgun by the wrong end and shot himself instead . . . the ribald raiders who couldn't get away because their getaway car had been *towed* away . . . the hopeless hold-up man who wrote his demand note on the back of his business card . . . tragic victims all, bowed in shame not just before the beak but in front of their fellow crooks as well. Prison, for them, is the least of their disgrace. As Napoleon once said: 'It is worse than a crime – it is a blunder.'

Don't Move, this is a cock-up

A give-away

Armed with a toy gun, Belfast bandit Kevin Lynch fired a blank in his sales counter hold-up.

For starters, the staff had nothing to sell – they were giving it all away. And precisely what they were giving away were the day's newspapers. Reams of them.

Finally convinced there wasn't a penny in the till, Lynch fled, leaving behind his coat which contained his address and the number of the prison cell he had left hours before.

Lynch staged his hold-up at the newspaper office where he once worked. But he did not know that because of a strike, the paper was being given away free.

At Ulster Crown Court the judge, Mr Justice Murray, opined 'This may not have been the great train robbery, or as well organised, but it was still a serious crime.'

Said his defence lawyer: 'It was ludicrous, inept and bizarre.'

Cut and thrust

Nothing went right the day Charlie Watts held up a post office with a toy pistol.

As he reached across the counter to grab £3,600 in banknotes he smashed the protective glass screen and cut his hand.

Then, as he made good his escape, the cardboard box he'd put the money in split in the street and he lost most of his haul.

At the Old Bailey prosecutor Mr Edward Laskey said, 'It was like a Chaplin comedy.'

81

Caught on the hop

Bungling burglar Phillip McCutcheon's dream of becoming a master criminal was doomed from the start.

The judge told him so in no uncertain terms, pointing out that with only one leg, a glass eye and a deformed hand his chances of success were somewhat limited, to say the least.

He cannot climb drainpipes, or run from the law. His sight is impaired, and he can only use his good hand to help himself to other people's property.

Indeed, as police pointed out after one farcical escapade, his handicaps have helped to make him one of Britain's easiest villains to catch.

At York Crown Court, recorder Mr Rodney Percy delivered the most withering admonition of McCutcheon's inabilities.

'You are a rotten burglar. You are always being caught and are always in trouble.

'You have been caught in Otley, Leeds, Harrogate, Norfolk, Beverley, Hull, York – the lot. It's time you gave up, isn't it?'

And, went on Mr Percy, 'Whoever heard of a burglar succeeding with only one leg, something wrong with one hand, and a glass eye? You haven't a hope of getting away with it, not a hope, and yet you are still doing it.'

What Mr McCutcheon was doing at the time of his arrest in 1977 was trying to drive a car while unfit through drink and drugs.

The offence, which involved hitting two parked cars, and was occasioned by the combined effects of a drinking bout and the drugs he was taking to ease the pain from his new artificial leg, had all the familiar elements of near-farce which characterised many of his previous escapades.

One of those involved breaking into a chicken coop and stealing eight hens. Police had no difficulty in tracking him down after finding his carving knife in the henhouse and four wishbones in his home.

Admitting the drink driving charge, for which he was fined £10 and banned from driving for a further six months, Mr McCutcheon explained that he had been born with a hand deformity, had to have his leg amputated because of bone disease, and lost his eye when a woman assaulted him.

Don't bet on it

When the race is on, and his horse is in there with a chance, there's no point trying to interest a gambling man in any other subject, no matter how persuasive your argument.

Which simple lesson in human psychology appears to have eluded the three desperadoes who raided a busy Plymouth bookmakers shop just as the big race was getting under way.

Masked in balaclavas, and waving guns, the trio shouted, 'Freeze! This is a hold-up.'

No-one paid a blind bit of notice. Too many customers were infinitely more concerned in the fortunes of a horse called Dodgy Future.

Faced with such disinterest, the three trousered their revolvers and left, not a penny the richer.

If it's any consolation to them, the punters didn't do so well either. Dodgy Future could only manage second place.

The raiders took about £600 in cash. 'They left nothing untouched, the whole place was a shabgm', selM'bolatetaoin in a shambles,' Mr Higgins said. – **From the North Berks Herald**

Reverse charge

Just about everything went wrong for the two would-be hold-up men who tried to steal a £28,000 wages delivery from a British Telecom office in North London.

For a start the men had been supplied with 'hopeless' information by their inside contact, canteen manageress Joyce Knott.

The offices were busier than usual, and the raiders, both of whom were carrying shotguns, had difficulty in forcing their way through the crowds.

The final blow came when they reached the wages office, only to find the door locked.

Detectives fell about laughing as the two men, still clutching their shotguns, started arguing over the bungled raid.

They were still laughing as they took away John Mann and Paul Halligan, to face conspiracy and firearm charges.

Raiders of the lost office

It was no mean feat of cinematographic ingenuity that enabled bosses at the famous Elstree Studios to foil two armed raiders who tried to hold up their wages office.

For the team that brought you *Star Wars* and *Raiders of the Lost Ark* had another special effect in store when the bungling duo swooped.

Unknown to the pair, studio chiefs switch the office every week to foil would-be hold-up attempts. When the gunmen strolled in behind security guards delivering the weekly wages, the change of script proved too much for them – they promptly got lost.

From then on the scenario turned to one of pure farce.

'It was like something out of the Ealing Comedies,' said managing director Andrew Mitchell.

'The raiders saw the security van outside and went to the office we used last week for wages. But it was empty.

'The men then attacked the door of another office with an axe, but the noise alerted staff.'

At which point, 'One of the raiders fired a pistol into the wall to warn them off, and they ran out empty-handed.'

Sacking offence

It should have been the world's biggest heist – £45 million worth of diamonds and other jewels stored in the head office vault of a Neapolitan pawnbrokers. Unfortunately the machine-gun gang needed 160 sacks to carry off their haul and they only brought nine.

They also had to ignore 8,000 safety deposit boxes because the guard with the key to the strongroom had gone for a coffee break and couldn't be found.

Still, the 14-man gang, dressed as surgeons, didn't do too

badly out of the night. After holding 60 employees at gun-point they made off with some £4 million.

In court he pleaded guilty to having an offensive weapon and pleaded not guilty to using insulting stomach of another man in the behaviour. — **From the Yorkshire Evening Post**

Stick 'em up

With 20 prison sentences behind him, Edward McAlea had had plenty of time to practise getting his criminal activities right.

But although he planned the raid on the watchmaker's shop with precision, it hardly went off like clockwork.

He burst into Mr Philip Barrett's Liverpool shop wearing a pair of women's tights over his head and brandishing a child's cap gun. But when he waved the gun under the noses of staff and customers and shouted: 'This is a stick-up,' nobody took him seriously.

This was hardly surprising as the 37-year-old Irishman had forgotten to take the protective cork out of the barrel of his toy gun.

As Mr Barrett and his customers chased McAlea out of the shop, the hapless villain panicked and whipped off his stocking mask. At which stage Mr Barrett recognised him as a customer who only the day before had sold him his watch for £11.

When police later found the tights, gun and two reels of caps at McAlea's home, he told them he had 'done it as a joke'.

The bodged-up stick-up, was described in court as 'a bungling amateurish incident, doomed to failure from the outset.'

Before sending him to prison for two-and-a-half years the judge heard that the Irishman had difficulty in reconciling himself to life outside his familiar prison walls.

Explained his defence counsel Mr Andrew McDonald: 'He's like a caged animal who goes wild when he's released.'

Helping with inquiries

Scolded for queue-jumping in a Glasgow bank, would-be robber William Gillen shuffled to the back of the queue and patiently waited his turn before handing over a demand note.

The teller, meanwhile, had sounded the alarm and Gillen

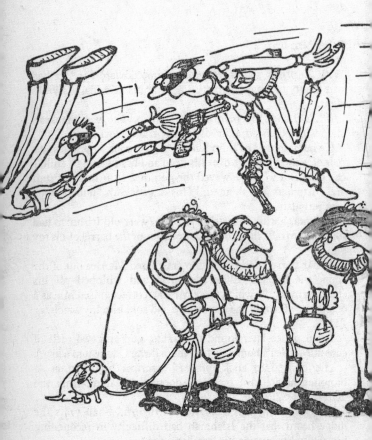

fled empty-handed, only to be arrested minutes later for shop-lifting.

Later, at a police identity parade, the bank teller failed to pick him out. Gillen shouted, 'Don't you recognise me.' His solicitor said: 'His only explanation for his conduct is craziness.'

Show stealers

Two hard-up art students got the idea of staging a raid while watching a comic robbery in the college pantomime. Their's turned out even more farcical.

They stole props from the show, including a home-made sawn-off shotgun, and set out to rob the Midland Bank in Maida Vale, North London.

One shouted, 'Fill up this bag with money or I'll blow your head off.'

But the gun began to fall apart, and as the other student robber tried to piece it together the teller rang the alarm bell.

The students panicked and fled empty-handed. As they ran off the gun exploded, shooting a hole through their carrier bag.

When they got back to their getaway car police were there ahead of them. The car was so badly parked, an officer was waiting to book the driver. He arrested them instead.

The judge at the Old Bailey heard the students planned to 'paint Paris red' with their takings.

They were told they would have to put off their planned visit for at least five years, however, while they pondered their folly in one of Her Majesty's prisons.

Thieves described by the police as 'amateurs' broke into the Shakespeare Memorial Theatre at Stratford-on-Avon, it was discovered yesterday morning, tried to steal a heavy steel safe witashea-prgtp ocmfw cmfwyp safe with a stage-property sword and a Shakespearean statue, smashed restaurant cupboard and disturbed bar stock. – **From *The Daily Telegraph***

Through a glass darkly

Thinly disguised in shocking pink gloves, dark glasses, a fur anorak and a yellow crash helmet which was still glistening with wet paint, Mark Poynton set out to rob a sub-post office where he was well known.

But owing to a combination of drink and the sunglasses he

tripped before he could reach the counter. Then, as he tried to snatch £300 from the till, the manager slammed it shut on his fingers.

As Poynton turned to flee a woman customer in the Hertfordshire post office clobbered him with a cushion. Others then joined in and sat on top of him until the police arrived.

Withdrawal symptoms

On the dole and feeling the pinch, Simon Bingley bought himself a 65p plastic gun and a joke mask with a red funny nose and big rubbery lips.

Thus equipped, he pulled off a £2,000 raid on the Cheltenham and Gloucester Building Society. He might have got away with it, too, had he not elected to hold up his local branch.

Despite the mask, staff at the Cowley office had no difficulty recognising him. He was, after all, one of their regular customers.

Weak ticker

Tellers in a New York bank froze in horror when a pint-sized Irishman placed a huge box on the counter and said, 'Dis is a bomb.'

And he warned he would detonate it unless staff did as he told them. He ordered one: 'Give me all your hundreds and fifties.'

Patrick McGill stuffed £1,500 in his pockets, picked up his cardboard box 'bomb' and headed for the door.

But just as the little Irishman reached it, burly security guard Joseph Bykowski stepped out to block his way and McGill fainted clean away.

Detectives had to summon oxygen to revive him so they could arrest him. A NYPD spokesman said, 'It's the craziest case we've ever had.'

Mr Wilkinson said he was then confronted by three men with stocking masks and iron bras – **From a local newspaper report.**

Wrong type

Two men who held up a video shop in West London were so thick they thought the typewriter on the counter was the till – and ordered the manager at gunpoint to 'open it up'.

Even when they spotted their mistake they managed to grab only £3 from the real till.

Then their shotgun went off accidentally scaring them so much that they fled, dropping the cash in the doorway in their haste to get away.

The catalogue of blunders was detailed at the Old Bailey, where one of the raiders, 19-year-old John Gregory, was given four years youth custody.

'This was an amateurish affair with a comic element,' said defence counsel Mr Ian Lee.

If a burglar boobs, or a bandit blows it, he can expect to end up before the court to answer for the error of his ways.

If he really fouls up the job he might even have to do a stretch in the intensive care unit before facing the judge.

Then there are the real unfortunates who manage to bypass the whole legal system, for their mistakes are fatal.

In which case they still have to account for their crimes – only before a higher seat of judgement. . . .

Horrors of the Black Museum

Deathly hush

On his first raid of the night a young burglar caused so much noise he awoke the householder and had to run off.

After that the night went steadily downhill.

On his second raid he again kicked up a rumpus, waking everyone in the house and, in his haste to escape, leapt through a closed window.

Police in Twickenham, South London, called to arrest him, had to give him a heart massage and apply a tourniquet instead, so badly cut was he by the jagged glass from the window through which he had tried to make his hasty exit.

His last words, just before he died in a policeman's arms, were about the only thing he got right all night – 'I'm bleeding fast.'

A losing hand

Fingerprint experts were not required at the scene of a bungled burglary in Nairobi, Kenya. The victim left his hand behind instead.

It was chopped off at the wrist by irate British businessman Mr Claude Robertson-Dunn, swinging a Japanese Samurai sword, who afterwards announced: 'Police are now looking for Kenya's one-armed bandit.'

***

The incident had a sequel a few weeks later when the hand was produced in court as prime exhibit and its owner, Nduini Kamere, was jailed for two years.

At the hearing police congratulated Mr Robertson-Dunn on his swift and summary action. He shrugged off the praise thus: 'There was no question of bravery. A good clean swipe and it was all over.'

The coroner warned the mother: 'Whether you think a child is dead or not, don't place it under a bucket in the garden in future.'
– **From the Hastings and St Leonard's Observer**

Box of tricks

All that glisters is not gold, as Robert Owen discovered to his cost when he raided a North Sea supply base.

The reason for his concern was that the small box he had handled during his raid at the Norwell Yard in Great Yarmouth was marked 'Radioactive'. A discovery which so terrified him that he gave himself up to police even though he had stolen nothing.

Doctors said the effects of contamination would not appear for five days, and magistrates heard that Owen had spent 'a very uncomfortable time praying nothing had happened'.

OOooooops!

Disturbed while burgling a flat at Colindale, North London, 23-year-old Sikiru Aderonmu leapt from a window to escape. He landed smack on top of his getaway car and died three days later from the injuries thus sustained.

Grief-case

The thief who lifted a briefcase from the back seat of a car in Sydney, Australia, probably didn't feel all that comfortable either after hearing what he'd got away with.

Police put out an urgent bulletin after the bio-medical engineer whose case it was explained what was inside, namely medical instruments contaminated with Hepatitis B and Acquired Immune Deficiency Syndrome (AIDS).

Dead-cert

Police were also rather anxious to track down the thieves who made off with a safe stolen from a vet's surgery at Cambourne, Cornwall.

The raiders thought it was crammed full of cash. In fact it contained twelve sealed boxes of the drug Immobilon, which is used to anaesthetise horses and is so dangerous that it has to be kept under lock and key.

Anxiety over the thieves' well-being followed a warning by the veterinary surgeon, Mr Denis Harvey, who explained, 'Just one drop of this drug on the skin can kill. My fear is that the thieves will blow open the safe and police will find their bodies.'

Death was due to strangulation due to asphyxiation caused by strangulation resulting from gagging. – **From the** *Evening News*

Finger of suspicion

The man who attempted a smash and grab raid on a travel agency in Barking, Essex, fled empty-handed in more ways than one.

For when the police turned up later to check for clues they found part of the raider's finger impaled on a piece of jagged glass.

Nearby hospitals were alerted in case the man sought medical attention. Forensic experts were confident the man would not be long in being caught because they had the raider's blood group and just about the best fingerprint imaginable.

Commented a police spokesman: 'The person responsible will be recognisable for life, and sooner or later someone will put the finger on him.'

Deadly cargo

'Drugs were his passport home,' said Londoner Reg Fuller about his 22-year-old son Ian.

'But', he added, 'It was a passport to death.'

Fuller swallowed 375 capsules of heroin in India and successfully smuggled them through customs at Heathrow. But some burst in his stomach, and he died in agony.

Coroner Dr Paul Knapman warned other would-be stomach smugglers, 'Your intimate body search might be by a pathologist in a mortuary.'

Haynes might even have killed his nephew and people had got to learn that the use of knives, even on relatives, would not be tolerated. – From the *Richmond and Twickenham Times*

Death mask

Interviewed about his murder squad's failure to identify the body of an armed robber who was accidentally shot by one of his fellow thieves while raiding a bank in Limerick, a Garda spokesman said, 'The fact that a number of detectives saw the corpse but could not put a name to it is understandable if you bear in mind that it was still masked.'

Skullduggery

Found lying drunk in a gutter clutching a woman's skull in a bag, James Walkden told police: 'I stole it from the cemetery to put on top of my TV for decoration.'

After hearing that Walkden had been out on the town and had stolen the skull, which belonged to a woman who had been buried 27 years earlier, magistrates at Darwen, Lancashire, fined him £50. He was also sacked from his job on the grounds that he had betrayed his employer's trust.

At the time of the incident Walkden worked as a cemetery attendant.

It's a Fair Cop

This time-honoured expression originated among Cockney criminals. Loosely translated, it means: 'You're quite right, officer. It was I who perpetrated this felony. Kindly slip the handcuffs on and lead me to your cells.'

Over the years it has gained more popular usage, still signifying: 'Fair deal. No argument.'

It is also applied willy-nilly to women police officers. There is not a tabloid journalist under the Sun who can resist the phrase when writing about a WPC, regardless of whether the lady in question is indeed fair, or has a face like the back of a black maria.

It's a Fair Cop

Give and take

Thieves who broke into a house in Bogor, West Java, were perturbed to find a policeman's uniform hanging in a cupboard they were in the process of rifling. After returning to their original resting places the various items they had planned to steal, they slipped quietly out of the house leaving behind a note which read: 'Sorry, Sir, we mistakenly entered and we guarantee that none of your things were stolen.' Then they broke into the house next door and stole a tape recorder, an amplifier, a watch and 2,400 baht in cash.

M.I.3½

Irish police conceded that they had a problem on their hands when one of their number managed to lose a van, loaded with top secret documents, while partaking of liquid refreshment at a Garda Siochana social club.

The difficulty arose because, although the police desperately wanted their van back, they were unable to issue a description of it to the people they were asking to help find it for them. It was, they explained, a Special Branch vehicle, and they didn't want the public to know what it looked like.

The other little problem was that odd items which went missing from the van, like secret documents detailing security arrangements at the British Embassy in Dublin and measures taken for the protection of Ulster judges and VIPs and Special Branch surveillance targets and such like, kept turning up on beaches and on waste ground beside golf courses. It was rather embarrassing.

It was somewhat embarrassing, too, for the police chorister who had borrowed the van for a night out.

It emerged that the van was being used to transport the Special Branch files to an incinerator. Unfortunately, the

incinerator was not working properly, and six out of a dozen bags of documents due for burning were left in the vehicle.

The Garda chorister then used the van for choir business, but got side-tracked in the Garda club. He left the licenced premises in the early hours of the morning to find it gone.

A frantic search at dumping grounds for stolen vehicles turned up some of the bags of documents. Others were found on a beach, and near the Royal Dublin golf course.

The case of the missing van followed several other equally embarrassing instances involving the theft of policemen's uniforms. The thefts were attributed to Ireland's most wanted man, Dominic McGlinchey, and the joke doing the rounds at the time had the Irish Police Chief, Commissioner Larry Wren, quoted as saying: 'I hope he has found one to fit him.'

May the force be with me

As a conscientious officer, PC Alan Godfrey always reported any strange comings or goings in his patch.

So when one night he observed a UFO at Todmorden, West Yorks, he duly logged the event.

And he told how he had been beamed aboard the flying saucer, where he met eight small robots and 'a tall humanoid'.

Naturally the close encounter won him fame. It also lost him his job, PC Godfrey claimed when he was retired as medically unfit.

'I think I became an embarrassment to the force. They just wanted me out,' he explained.

Trigger finger

His escape route blocked by a detective, crouched in the classic marksman's stance, an armed raider at Palmer's Green, North London, threw down his gun and surrendered. Too late he discovered that the officer's 'weapon' was nothing more than a carefully aimed finger.

I want to be Bobby's guy

It was only when the young Chelsea bobby went straight that the trouble started.

Before that he had been a truly bent copper . . . bent in the gay sense, that is. For months he and a fellow officer in the same station had been lovers.

Their's was a story of stolen moments between patrols; of secret looks exchanged across a crowded courtroom.

Then into their life and station came a young and lovely woman PC. From that moment on, one man's interest in the gay life waned.

He chatted her up. He invited her out. Pretty soon he was head over heels in love with the fair cop. They talked of marriage and mortgages. It was that serious. It was even more serious for his jilted partner, who, in a fit of pique and jealousy, told all to their station chief.

But after sorting out the infernal triangle Scotland Yard ruled that all three should keep their jobs. The straight man, though, was transferred to another station.

A senior officer said, 'Action is usually taken only if there is conduct likely to bring the force into disrepute.'

Off-beat bobby

'We went wanging down there, jumped out of the van and just started fighting . . . it was a great day out, fighting the Pakis. It ought to be an annual fixture. I thoroughly enjoyed myself.' – London Police Constable recalling the July 1981 Southall disturbances, quoted in the Policy Studies Institute's 1983 report on the Metropolitan Police Force.

Dog's dinner

A court in Wolverhampton allowed a police witness to give evidence without his notes after the red-faced constable explained that his dog had eaten them.

The trial continued after magistrates agreed that he could

read from a statement he prepared from the notes before they were devoured.

'I am very embarrassed,' said PC Andrew Bevington.

Double take

As they cased the joint prior to a bit of breaking and entering, a chilling realisation dawned on the two burglars. *They were not alone!*

Two other shadowy figures were also lurking about. 'We've been rumbled. It's the law,' said the two burglars, one to another.

Meanwhile exactly the same thought had occurred to the aforesaid two shadowy figures, for they were also burglars.

There followed a glorious interlude of pure farce as each pair tried to dodge the other. At length they came face to face, whereupon one villain, wielding an iron bar, challenged his opposite number: 'Are you CID?'

'No', came the offended reply. 'We thought you were.'

Their little misunderstanding all cleared up, the two pairs joined forces to raid the Widden Old Boys Rugby Club in Gloucester. But all the activity attracted some more shadowy figures – only this time it was the law, and all four crooks were collared.

The police arrested two IRA leaders, David O'Connell and Joe O'Neill, after an IRA funeral later today, but that appeared to be connected to a souffle during the funeral. – From the International Herald Tribune

Dab hand nab

After his preliminary inspection of a burgled house, a Scotland Yard forensic expert decided to test for fingerprints.

It was at this embarrassing point he discovered that his fingerprint kit had been stolen from his unmarked police van parked outside.

When he went to call for assistance, he couldn't. Someone had nicked the radio too.

The kit was later found discarded a few hundred yards away in Stoke Newington, North London. But before the expert could examine the burgled house he first had to fingerprint his own van. Scotland Yard withheld the victim's name to spare his blushes.

In a fix

Police in Palma, Majorca, arrested a mugger who snatched a Swedish girl tourist's handbag and ran off with it. Finding the recovered handbag stuffed full of heroin and other drugs, they promptly arrested the victim of the attack as well!

Robin hoodwinked

While driving through the Hyson Green red light district of Nottingham, Herbert Hoare was deeply moved by the looks of a young woman he spotted walking alone.

Hoare immediately drove to the nearest bank, collected £10 from its cash dispenser, and returned to offer it to her.

It was at this point she revealed herself to be WPC Janet Greenwood, on an undercover mission to catch kerb crawlers. Hoare's excuse, that she was 'a particularly attractive lady', did not impress Nottingham magistrates, who bound him over for a year.

Ring of confidence

It was a gem of a ring, a great big diamond and sapphire sparkler, and it fairly caught the eye of raider Stan Parkes.

Alas for him, his ever-loving took a shine to it too. Soon, the £400 ring was never off her hand. She wore it to the shops, in the street, everywhere.

And then one not very bright day Mrs Parkes wore it to Preston Crown Court, Lancashire. That was the day her husband was manfully denying he laid a finger on the ring, or anything else stolen in the £2,700 raid.

Until his wife, Ruby, turned up to lend support, 33-year-old Parkes had a fighting chance of getting off the charge.

But the ring shone out like a beacon to wronged owner John Boardman. He told police, the trial was halted, and before long Mrs Parkes was back in court.

Only this time around she was ringless and standing in the dock beside her husband. For his part, Parkes had changed his plea to guilty – 'because of his wife's astonishing foolishness,' the prosecution claimed.

Caught in the door

There's an old Anglo-Irish joke about building sites always being deserted on Thursday because that's the day all the unemployed building workers go to collect their dole money.

The out-of-work Welshman who agreed to help his son start up as a locksmith would have understood this only too well after going along to help with the first job.

This entailed fixing doors at the Social Security Office in Bridgend, Mid Glamorgan, where he had been claiming sickness benefit. After being visited by DHSS investigators he wisely agreed to drop his claim.

Vice-versa

The Galaxy massage parlour on Dublin's North Circular Road insisted on certain standards of decorum.

'There was no full sexual intercourse,' Supt. William Herlihy told the Circuit Criminal Court.

But for a tenner, clients could have a shower, hand relief and a hard porn film. 'Topless relief massage' cost an extra £4; the 'full frontal strip relief' was £20, and at £26 there was oral sex.

The police raid on the Galaxy cost owner Thomas Quinn dearly. He was fined £80, and lost his job – as a vice squad detective.

Under the Influence

The worst thing about getting absolutely, monumentally blotto is that the next day you have to explain away all the daft things you did.

Generally you do your explaining to some stony-faced, stone-cold-sober soul like your wife or loved one. Or, if you have really enjoyed yourself, to a magistrate. You do not expect much understanding.

There ought to be a law about this. We reckon the wife/loved one/judge, whoever, should get equally legless before sitting in judgement upon you.

That way he/she/it will doubtless understand that what you did seemed a good idea at the time.

Until that bright day dawns we offer you the following sobering thoughts.

Under the Influence

What a whopper

After a night's drinking spree, two Welshmen were amazed to find a 14-ft dinosaur crouching by the roadside.

Rather than leave it there they decided to take it home for their children to see.

After staggering a mile along the way with the dinosaur on their shoulders they were halted by a police dog handler.

At first they attempted to bluff it out. When asked where they were going with the dinosaur, they replied 'What dinosaur?'

Pressed further, they challenged the officer that if he could, indeed, see a dinosaur, he should get his dog to attack it.

Instead he arrested the two men and took the dinosaur, made of fibreglass and stolen earlier that evening from an amusement park, into police custody.

The high-spirited pair were cleared of theft, but ordered to pay compensation for the dinosaur's injuries, sustained when it fell on top of them.

Unarmed combat

Enraged by the fisherman who kept grinning at him, John Wilson challenged, 'Who do you think you're laughing at?'

But the 6-ft tall fisherman, clad in yellow oilskins and sou'wester, just went right on smiling.

Wilson took a swipe at him, and knocked his arm clean off his body. At which point he caught on that the 'fisherman' who was standing outside a fish and chip shop in Chester was, in fact, a fibreglass dummy.

In defence it was admitted that Wilson was several sheets to the wind at the time.

Com-raid

A young Soviet burglar with an ear for music hit a sour note when he broke into a flat in the city of Baku, on the Caspian Sea. He filled two sacks with valuables and then decided to take a bath before leaving.

After completing his ablutions he felt peckish, so he fixed himself a meal in the flat's well-appointed kitchen. Then he helped himself to a bottle of Vodka, and settled down to enjoy the feast.

Thus satisfied, and by now feeling warm, contented and slightly mellow, not to mention considerably richer, he prepared to make good his departure. It was at this point that his eye chanced upon a piano in the corner.

Unable to resist the temptation, he placed the two sacks containing the valuables on the floor, hung his jacket over the back of a chair, and began to play and sing.

As he warmed to the keyboard the strange sounds emanating from the supposedly empty flat prompted neighbours to call the police, who arrived while he was in full song and arrested him.

It is not often that a burglar comes across a house, or indeed business premises, that is properly protected with burglar-proof tail canapes. The Hungarians use it in much greater quantity to give its mild flavour to goulashes and chicken dishes. – **From the *Nottinghamshire Free Press***

Blow by blow account

Having failed to supply a breath sample, a Bristol motorist challenged Judge Anthony Bulger to try his luck on the test machine.

M'learned judge fluffed it too, commenting he 'ran out of huff and puff'.

But he still found 19-year-old Ronald Dawson guilty. He had 'no reasonable excuse', quoth his worship.

The wonder of woolies

It was the night before Christmas and outside the streets were all aglow.

Inside an otherwise deserted Woolworth's, the tramp was fairly well lit up too.

And for the next four days, while staff took their Christmas break, he minded the store, gloriously full of the festive spirit.

He was in much the same condition when salesgirls returned to prepare for the New Year sales. They found him snoring away in the bedding department, surrounded by empty whisky and cider bottles.

As he slept off his binge in police cells at Portsmouth, staff worked out he had knocked back £38 worth of drink, plus the odd Mars bar, some Smarties, and a little Turkish Delight.

One employee said: 'The man was in no fit state to make his escape when we returned.'

Open and shut case

Alarm bells rang out in the middle of the night as a burglar raided a do-it-yourself store at Chesterfield, Derbyshire.

Flinging open a door to escape, he found himself confronted by a blank wall. In mounting panic he tried eleven more, all with the same result.

The doors were part of a special DIY display.

Eventually he found an escape route, but in his haste to get away he tumbled down a flight of stairs and knocked himself out. Police found him there, still unconscious, the following morning.

A police spokesman said: 'He had been drinking and made a right mess of it.'

Coarse fishing

The midnight streets of Birmingham were singularly devoid of trout, perch and carp. But a trifle like that did nothing to dim Craig Allen's sudden passion for a spot of fishing.

Staggering somewhat from the effect of his night's drinking

116

spree, he assembled his rod and pushed it through the letter-box of a ladies' lingerie shop.

One quick flick of the wrist and he had a bite. He reeled in his catch – a sexy pink bra. Moments later, watching police officers were reeling in Allen.

At Birmingham Crown Court, where he was fined £40, Allen said, 'It's amazing what you'll do when you're skiffy.'

The breathalyser has been criticised as inaccurate, but it is merely a quick screening device, and those who give a positive reaction then have either a blood or a wine test. – **From the** *Belfast Newsletter*

Disorganised crime

The mastermind of the Great Organ Robbery did not quite pull out all the stops. In fact he even forgot to pull out the plug.

So he gave police an easy lead on the heist.

Bemused officers chanced upon the two robbers in the wee small hours, pushing the electric organ up a street in Rugby, Warwickshire.

One man was dressed like comic Max Wall in a bald wig, black tights and big boots. He rapidly legged it.

Behind the organ trailed an extension cable leading all the way back to the shop from where it had been stolen.

His companion, David Bale, fined £50 for handling the organ, explained that he and the mystery man had been to a fancy dress party, where they had consumed vast quantities of strong alcohol.

His defence council said 'Getting into dishonest trouble was the last thing on his mind.'

Tea and sympathy

There was only one place where out-of-work odd-job man Terry O'Neill felt really safe – and that was in prison.

So after tramping the streets of Lewes, East Sussex, in

search of somewhere to stay he decided to break *into* prison to find a bed for the night.

But he was spotted as he climbed back over the prison wall the next morning.

In court, charged with stealing a kettle, a jar of coffee and a box of tea-bags labelled 'Property of Her Majesty's Prison', he told magistrates, 'I didn't feel safe in the streets, what with all this crime. I thought the prison would provide a sort of sanctuary.

'And,' he added 'very comfortable it was too. It had all the amenities – there was even an electric fire to keep me warm.'

O'Neill admitted scaling the prison wall, breaking into a workman's hut and stealing goods worth £20.

But he was given a 12-month conditional discharge after telling the court he had drunk seven pints of beer and had acted 'on the spur of the moment'.

Shurely shome mishtake

Two drunkards Sri P. Appa Rao, a railway employees and another person Sri T, Ramana Rao, a railway employee living at Kahrida with a friendly relation. On 22.9.84 both were plunged into drunkerness and started non-sense talks. The non-sense talks later lead to a serious brawl. Sri Appa Rao hit Sri Ramana Rao by a lathi which caused instantaneous death. Suddenly a gloominess cast its shadow in the house of Ramana Rao. – **From a report in the Indian Newspaper,** *Swadhin Patrika*

P . . . p . . . pick up a p . . . p . . . penguin

He took it, he said, for a lark.

Odd thing to do really. It was nothing like a lark. It was a rather rare Humboldt penguin, worth £600 and answering to the name of Percy.

But David Worsley was not aware of this. He was hardly aware of anything – having just downed eight pints of beer, eight shots of rum and two bottles of cider in a drinking contest.

It was in this exalted state that he climbed a fairground big dipper, tumbled off and fell to earth in Southport Zoo, slap bang beside the penguin pen.

That was when he first clapped eyes on Percy. It was love at first sight.

Worsley picked up the penguin, tucked him in a wire rubbish bin as a makeshift cage, and staggered off into the night.

Then he thought what a jolly jape it would be if his pal were to open his car boot and find a penguin giving him the old beady eye.

So Percy, who seems to have been an easy going bird, went into the boot. Worsley's mate was rather more ruffled when he found out.

'At first he thought it was funny,' the penguin pincher told police later. 'But then he wasn't happy about it.'

Worsley's mum got into even more of a flap when he told her. Take it back, she ordered. Right away.

Worsley obeyed, even though he and Percy were getting on like a house on fire. He recalled: 'I became very fond of the little fellow and used to pat him on the head.'

'He seemed very tame and sat on my lap all the way back to Southport.'

In a seafront car park, not far from the zoo, the pair parted. Worsley left Percy in a largish bucket, cosily lined with straw. He thoughtfully tipped it on its side so the penguin could waddle off home.

And Percy did waddle off, but whither he waddled no one knows to this day. Even a sea and land search failed to pick up the penguin.

When Worsley heard his little playmate had not shown up he became so distressed he went to the police and told all.

But there was scant sympathy, and when he duly appeared before the beak he was fined £100 plus £600 compensation for poor old Percy.

The sorry affair also cost him emotionally. Afterwards Worsley confessed: 'I can't sleep at night for thinking about Percy.'

Own Goals

In the early, hairy days of the present Ulster troubles, bombs were altogether more primitive affairs than now.

Timing devices ranged from alarm clocks, through condoms to clothes pegs. Often bombs failed to go off bang on time, so to speak.

This resulted in several embarrassing incidents involving unfortunate desperadoes blowing themselves up, instead of other people. The Army, with mordant humour, described such events as Own Goals.

There were many variations of the Own Goal.

One classic case involved a brace of Provos planting a bomb outside an office block. While one primed it, the other kept watch. Then onto the scene strolled a curious cat. It pussyfooted up behind the primer, rubbed itself against his legs, and purred.

The IRA man stepped back, swung a kick at the cat, missed, kicked the bomb, killed the cat, *and* himself, and blew his mate's leg off.

Not all own goals have such explosive results, although your average common-or-garden criminal has the unhappy knack of putting his foot in it too.

Own Goals

Breech of contract

Things were looking bleak indeed for Terry Whitlock as his trial neared an end. With every passing day the prospect of a seven year stretch loomed ever larger.

The way he saw it, his only hope of a lenient sentence lay in winning the judge's sympathy and there wasn't much hope of that.

And then Whitlock had his harebrained idea. He put out a contract on himself. It was not a very big contract, you understand, just £100. But Whitlock didn't want himself wasted. All he needed was a nice little kneecapping job.

That way, he figured, he could limp into court on crutches, his leg swathed in bandages and the judge would let him off lightly.

So much for the plan. It was the execution of it that went haywire. Whitlock found himself a hit-man called Arthur and gave him the £100.

He explained to Arthur that he was a bit squeamish about seeing himself be shot, so, would Arthur sort of sneak up on him sometime, and shoot him from behind.

Arthur, apparently a man of some sensitivity, agreed.

Came the night before the trial ended and Whitlock went off to the pub with some friends. As he staggered off home Arthur suddenly struck.

And there's no denying that he gave value for money. From point blank range he loosed off a shotgun, blasting a two-inch hole in Whitlock's leg. In hospital they dug 33 pellets out of the wound and pronounced Whitlock lucky to be alive. He would have a permanent limp.

There was even worse to follow. Instead of the expected sympathy Whitlock ended up facing another trial, this time for conspiring to pervert the course of justice.

Prosecutor Warwick McKinnon told an Old Bailey jury, 'The execution of the shooting by Arthur was a botched job.

Whitlock lost a lot of blood and at one stage his life was in danger.'

Trouble glazing

Police at Ruislip, Middlesex, were called when a burglar tried to break *out* of a house. Michael Duffy trapped himself in and when the law arrived he was smashing chairs against the reinforced glass windows in a vain bid to escape.

In the can

Between them, in just one year, the four gunmen had starred in more gangster movies than Edward G Robinson.

And the box office takings were generous – £137,000 in 35 raids on building society offices in London.

But unknown to them the gang was filmed by security cameras in no less than 13 of the robberies.

After screening the rushes Scotland Yard knew enough about their methods to seize Alexander Donnelly, David Smith, Dorian Joseiah and Anthony Dowse.

Underdone

Police caught thief Basil Lamb red-handed *and* blue-legged.

When stopped by a detective near London's Smithfield meat market, the 36-year-old butcher was shivering uncontrollably. He could hardly speak, his teeth were chattering so much.

Closer investigation revealed the reason – a stolen 3lb fillet of frozen beef tucked down his trouser leg.

Tricky combination

The young woman freed by firemen at Van Huys, California, in 1971 had some tricky explaining to do when her boss arrived on the scene. She had her arm stuck in his safe.

Guard duty

While South Yorkshire police were warning householders to be on their guard against burglars, the thieves struck again . . . at the home of Chief Constable James Brownlow.

Half-baked

Bungling burglar Harrry Savage didn't fare much better either. He had to telephone police and ask them to come and rescue him after he broke into a bakery in Leeds, Yorkshire, and got locked in. Magistrates gave him a conditional discharge upon hearing that he was out of work and homeless.

Mugged

There was one unsung band that turned up regularly at all the big summer rock festivals. The nine men and a girl who made up the outfit preferred to remain undiscovered.

For their's was a band of thieves, looting the tents of rock fans while the big names were on stage.

At the three-day Reading Festival, the gang pinched some 300 bits and pieces, worth £12,000. They used four tents and three cars to cache their hoard of cameras, portable TVs and the like.

The show would have gone off without a hitch but for a slip-up on the part of one careless member of the gang. As a result of which the whole haul was recovered after one fan spotted his stolen coffee mug outside the gang's tent.

Child's play

Next time maybe he'll just stay home and say he's got a headache.

Wine store boss Richard Otlet certainly ended up with one the last time he ducked his girlfriend's invitation to the school play she was producing.

In advance he arranged for the landlord of his local pub to phone, saying Richard's shop had just been burgled.

It worked a treat. While teacher Jacki Williams went on with the show, Richard was at home in Bristol chortling over his wizard wheeze.

Then came another phone call about the burglary . . . and a third. Exasperated detectives finally had to knock on his door to convince him his shop really *had* been burgled.

Still, he didn't have to watch Jacki's pupils perform *A*

Midsummer Night's Dream. But Richard's own playacting wasn't so wonderful either. Ruefully admitting his folly afterwards, he said, 'It became a nightmare.'

Listen here. . .

Demonstrating to a potential buyer a radio he had just stolen the thief was less than amused when the New York station he had tuned in to broadcast a description of himself.

The 'buyer' held the thief – and the radio – until the police arrived to arrest him.

Lost and fined

The day she took a train trip to Portsmouth, a 43-year-old woman certainly hit a losing streak.

First she lost her handbag after leaving it in a carriage.

Then she lost her marbles when she 'phoned to see if anyone had found it.

For inside the bag was £120 in forged £20 notes, all with the same serial number.

Police couldn't believe their luck when the woman turned up to collect it.

Cheque mate

Golfer Ian Harvey chipped and putted his way to the 19th hole, blissfully unaware that back in the clubhouse someone was rifling his cheque book.

It might have taken him weeks to find out that the thief had stolen a single cheque from the back of the book.

But the very next morning, when he was back at work as a bank teller, the evidence presented itself, along with thief Shaun Summers.

An astonished Mr Harvey found himself asked to cash his own cheque for £45 with his carefully forged signature on it. Recovering from his surprise, he had Summers arrested on the spot.

The thief later told police he had stolen five cheques, all from different players, during a bank-organised golf tournament. He copied the owners' signatures from comments in the club's suggestions book.

His one slip-up came when he failed to link the name on the cashier's desk with the name he had forged on the cheque.

Explaining his locker-room thefts, Summers told police, 'I was angered by the snobbery there. I did it to get back at some of the worst snobs.'

Blarney stoned

Sacked from a Midlands building site, the Irish labourer set out to wreak his revenge . . . in a hijacked JCB digger.

Trouble was, he was too sozzled to drive it. And the only other thing that ended up smashed was Liam O'Malley's own car when he ploughed into it, causing hundreds of pounds of damage.

Fired with enthusiasm

Part-time fireman Geoff Bell hadn't reckoned on the quick reactions of his fellow officers when he made a hoax alarm call to his own fire station at Fleet, Hampshire.

He was still on the phone when the officer answering his call activated the station crews' pocket bleepers to warn them of the 'emergency'.

As the bleepers went off all over town, so too did Bell's – its unmistakeable tone played straight back down the open telephone line to the fire station, where it was clearly heard by the officer at the other end.

Later a recording of his voice was recognised by his colleagues, and Bell was sacked from his part-time job with the local brigade.

'I'd had a few drinks with some mates in a pub,' said Bell after being fined £50 in court at Aldershot. 'It was a stupid thing to do.'

Fallen idle

His own defence counsel pronounced the most savage sentence on burglar Arthur Legge: 'The public has been well served by fate. He will never commit another crime.'

Legge, 27, from Catford, South East London, dived from a second floor balcony when cornered by police. He broke an arm and a leg, shattered his heel, and damaged his spine.

Said his lawyer: 'A minor fall could now cripple him completely.'

Mis-cast

A burglar fleeing after a raid on the home of Electric Light Orchestra star Jeff Lynne didn't have a leg to stand on after his getaway car crashed.

He was not only a bit unsteady after that, he also had one leg in plaster from a previous accident. He and his partner ended up having to phone a friend for a lift.

Banged to rights

While fooling around with a flick knife, a young beat bobby somehow managed to trip himself up.

And then, in the time-honoured phrase, 'his head came into contact with a police truncheon.' His own actually. He knocked himself out.

But that was just the start of PC Graham Parkin's troubles.

On waking up he made an emergency distress call on his police radio. He had been attacked, he said, by a man with a knife. He had been beaten unconscious.

And, sure enough, when a squad car raced to the scene, they found a singularly groggy PC Parkin lying in the grounds of a school.

Now it just so happened that earlier that night an off-licence had been raided just round the corner.

Detectives immediately linked the two incidents and deduced that a vicious, knife wielding, bobby-bashing, off-licence-raiding desperado was on the loose.

They set up a special incident room. A team of 31 officers got to work. They spent hundreds of hours interviewing Known Criminals, Taking Statements, that sort of thing.

They told the Press they were hunting a dangerous criminal.

And somewhat overawed by all this publicity, the man who raided the off-licence gave himself up. He wanted them to know he was an honest crook, not one of these knifeman maniacs you read so much about.

Some further police questioning of the battered bobby elicited the confession that he had knocked himself out, but had been too embarrassed to admit it.

The whole sorry tale ended, as did Parkin's 10-year police career, at York magistrates' court, where he was fined £200 for wasting his colleagues' time.

Money talks

As they ran off after their raid on a grocer's shop, two teenage burglars were most concerned to note an electronic screech emitting from the cashbox they had just stolen.

Too late they realised that the cashbox was, in fact, a burglar alarm. After trying to silence the device by jumping up and down on it and kicking it, they finally gave up and threw it into a passing river.

But the alarm had already done its job and the culprits were duly apprehended.

Trigger un-happy

Of course, Own Goals are not confined to villains, as the three members of the Spanish Security forces who landed in hospital after a shoot-out in a crowded disco can testify.

The three – two plainclothes detectives and a similarly plainclothed member of the para-military Civil Guard – were wounded after mistaking each other for terrorists and blazing away with their guns.

The embarrassing incident occurred in the town of Victoria, capital of the strife-torn Basque region, when the three detectives challenged two young men who were said to be armed and acting suspiciously.

Before the two groups were able to effect the necessary introductions one of the young men drew a gun and fired, injuring two of the policemen before he himself was shot and overpowered. Whereupon he identified himself and his companion as policemen from a different force who had themselves been called to the disco to check up on the other three.

'It was all a terrible misunderstanding,' a police spokesman said afterwards by way of explanation.

Wheels of Misfortune

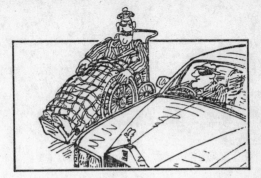

The Wheel of Fortune, like Fate's fickle finger, turns in many mysterious ways. For most of us it's a leisurely drive down the straight and narrow; but for our blundering heroes, more often than not it's a highspeed dash to disaster.

Wheels of Misfortune

Lame excuse

Alerted by the tinkling of falling glass, Glasgow police swooped on smash and grab raider Jimmy McFarlane.

They found him racing down the street, pushing a wheelchair containing his innocent friend and a stolen TV set. After a 400-yard chase they cornered the getaway vehicle.

His solicitor explained that McFarlane was pushing his invalid friend back from a party when he was inspired to smash a shop window and steal the TV. He then dumped it in the wheelchair and, pushing his charge and the proceeds of the raid in front of him, set off down the street.

Solicitor Ross Harper told the court, 'In London they use Rolls Royces but the Glasgow criminal prefers something less conspicuous. Maybe he thought no-one would connect a non-motorised wheelchair with a smash and grab raid.'

Sex appeal

Randy Al Hamburg made a love pact with his girlfriend. He told her: 'If you make love to me 50 times you can have my car.'

To keep score, he gave her a chart with 50 squares on it. Every time they had sex he would award her a gold star to stick on the chart. And he repeated his promise, 'When every square is filled you can keep my car.'

But after 33 lovemaking sessions – some in bed and some in the back of the car – the girl told Al she was 'too tired' to carry on.

When he protested, and reminded her of their pact, she drove off in the car and refused to give it back.

Angry Al took his unnamed mistress to court in Torrington, Wyoming, claiming breach of contract. The case was thrown out.

Afterwards Al, now left with no car, no girl and only 33 golden memories to sustain him, said he would appeal.

What a load of bullocks. . . .

. . . Or words of a similar sentiment must have occurred to
Cliff Ryder the night he drove a stolen car right into the
middle of a herd of cattle.

It would not have been the first time that night he felt so
moved. There had been that nasty moment when he triggered
the alarm while trying to burgle a social club at East Garston,
in Bedfordshire. And afterwards, when he suffered the
ignominy of falling through a window while escaping.

Things didn't get any better. After driving the car halfway
across England, Ryder had pangs of conscience and decided
to return it to its owner.

But on the long road home the car ran out of petrol. Ryder
abandoned it and hitched a lift to Scotland, where he was

promptly arrested trying to break into a house.

It was, Newbury magistrates were told, a singularly bun-gled night of crime.

Cab-nab

If the truncheon-wielding villain lived by any motto, it was: 'Help yourself'. Trouble was he did it once too often.

He helped himself to his victim's jewels, her money and anything else worth pinching. Then he helped himself to her car as a getaway vehicle.

Then, having loaded the boot with booty, he helped himself to her liquor. He had a large vodka . . . and another . . . and another.

By now he couldn't even manage to start the car, let alone drive it away. He unloaded it, 'phoned for a taxi and had another drink or two while he waited.

When the cab arrived he merrily began piling his loot into it. But the driver became suspicious and alerted the police at Finchley, North London, where our villain – by this time somewhat the worse for wear – was soon helping with their inquiries.

On yer bike

The painting that a man stole from an art gallery in Dulwich, South London, was worthy of something better.

It was, after all a £200,000 Rembrandt, which qualified it for a rather more upmarket getaway vehicle than the humble bicycle that was used.

Police afterwards gave this account of the daring daylight robbery:

A young man went into the Dulwich Gallery, where £10 million worth of paintings were on view, and made his way to a portrait of a man named Jacob de Gheyn, painted by the Old Master in 1669.

He lifted the 11 x 9 inch painting from the wall and put it in a shopping bag.

Then he calmly walked out of the main entrance, got on

his bike, and pedalled furiously away.

When guards noticed the Rembrandt missing they raised the alarm, raced out to their car and set off in pursuit. They caught up with the thief a mile away, panting and out of breath, and recovered the painting intact.

A police spokesman who confirmed afterwards that a man was helping them with their inquiries said, 'I should imagine this is the first time a Rembrandt has been stolen by a man on a bicycle.'

Finder's weepers

The painting, by now valued at a cool £1 million, was recovered in similarly farcical circumstances when it was again stolen some nine years later.

Police had little difficulty in tracking down the men responsible after they had tried to sell it back to the gallery from where it had been stolen in return for a £100,000 'finder's fee'.

The man who actually lifted the picture from the same Dulwich gallery, David Williams, told police after his arrest, 'I just wanted to nick a picture. I wouldn't have picked that one if I'd known it was so famous. I only knew it was valuable when I saw it on television.

'When I realised what it was I wanted to give it back,' he told the court in London before being jailed for three years.

Fatal flaw

A thief who stole an estate car in Warrington, Lancashire, abandoned it only half a mile away on discovering a coffin with a corpse in the back.

Boiled porridge

To facilitate a speedy getaway, bank robber Joseph Durning left the engine of his car running outside the White Lane,

Sheffield, branch of the Midland Bank.

But the robbery took so long to execute that while he was waiting for the right moment to vault over the counter and seize the contents of the till, the car's engine overheated, causing the water in the radiator to boil and drain away.

When he ran out of the bank, jumped into the car and attempted to drive away, the engine stalled, and Durning was captured.

During the past few days three bicycles have been stolen from Exeter streets. The police consider that a bicycle thief is at work.
- **From a report in the *Western Morning News***

Flash Harry

East Ender Anthony Douse lifted, among many other things, that immortal line first uttered by Bonnie and Clyde.

When a car dealer, intrigued by his big-spending habits, asked what he did for a living, Douse calmly replied: 'I rob banks.'

The salesman fell about laughing at the time. But later, when cars bought by Douse began figuring in a string of armed robberies, he remembered the funny customer and told the police.

Douse, it turned out, didn't exactly rob banks, but he did the next best thing by supplying getaway cars for a gang that did. Within hours of each raid he would turn up at showrooms, peeling off wads of banknotes to buy flash cars.

He started modestly by buying Ford Cortinas, but quickly worked his way up to a Cadillac, an Oldsmobile, a Range Rover and a nifty Lotus.

His part in the 10 raids, which netted £57,000, also earned him six years and nine months for conspiracy to rob.

A 17-year-old Copnor youth was remanded in custody to Portsmouth Quarter Sessions by Portsmouth Magistrates yester-

day after he had admitted stealing three bicycles, a record player,
thirty-one records, a National Insurance Card, and two cases of
false pretences. – Portsmouth Evening News

Driving ambition

Charged with 77 driving offences, David Tipper's fate was
sealed from the moment his solicitor stood up in court and
declared: 'If I were asked why these offences were committed I
would have difficulty in putting any reasons before you.'

Tipper, unemployed, of Eastville, Bristol, ran up his
amazing catalogue of blunders in 12 months of motoring
madness, during which time he was stopped by police 16
times and jumped bail twice.

When officers finally caught up with him he was driving
one of the 50 old bangers he had owned in the previous year.

Magistrates at Bristol heard that Tipper gave false names
to police, failed to produce driving documents, failed to
answer summonses, and failed to return to court after being
bailed. The list of charges took more than half-an-hour to read
out in court. After hearing that he had never passed a driving
test the magistrates fined him £469 for offences ranging from
having bald tyres to driving without due care and attention.
They also banned him from driving for three years after calcu-
lating that he had amassed an amazing 112 penalty points.

After the case Tipper explained: 'I was given the 50 cars.
They were all old bangers – what I would call disposable
cars.' He added: 'I'm not going to pay the fine.'

Police sergeant David Routlege told the court: 'It was no
surprise to me when he was arrested while driving a motor
vehicle. That seems to sum up his entire attitude for the past
year.'

Bicycle clips

Police called to arrest a cyclist staging a lone sit-down protest
in the middle of a busy Munich road had to call an ambulance
instead after he was run down and badly injured by a car. The

unnamed man was said to have staged his middle-of-the-road sit-in to protest against . . . motor traffic!

Positive lead

Puzzled by his car's failure to start, the motorist looked under the bonnet. With consternation he noted the battery was missing.

Police called to investigate the mystery found the battery safe and sound in it's usual resting place, under the rear passenger seat.

A Bedfordshire police spokesman reported, 'It was a case of assault and battery without the assault.'

Reverse-role

As getaway drivers go, Gary Ford didn't get very far. He couldn't even find the man he was supposed to help get away.

As he slowly cruised the streets of Ellesmere Port, Cheshire, looking for his partner in crime, he was flagged down by a couple of police officers.

They, too, were seeking his pal Anthony Austin after a £600 bag snatch, and asked Ford if he would oblige by giving them a lift while they combed the area.

Their error was short-lived. Both men were arrested soon afterwards and jailed.

Just the ticket

After a lifetime spent pulling the wool over the eyes of London's much-maligned traffic wardens, that most celebrated of socialites, Lady Diana Cooper, finally got her come-uppance after trying it on just once too often.

Notoriously bad at driving – her inability to steer a car was immortalised by Evelyn Waugh in his novel *Scoop* – Lady Diana's usual ruse when parking illegally on footpaths or double yellow lines is to attach a note to the windshield reading something like this: 'Dear Warden. Horribly old and frightfully lame. Have taken sad child to cinema – please forgive.'

On the occasion in question Lady Diana – a great beauty in her day, once worshipped by kings and toasted by Europe and now, in her 90s, still wry and sprightly – was on a shopping expedition to Harrods and had left her car outside with a note: 'Old cripple's car. Gone to lunch.'

Returning some time later she found a friendly note which read: 'Hope you had a good lunch, dear.' It was attached to a parking ticket.

SOD'S LAW: n. (vulg., & derog. or joc.) Law which decrees that if something can go wrong, it will. Can be applied especially to criminal blunderers, for whom it (something) invariably does (go wrong).

Sod's Law

Something borrowed, something blue

The 'something borrowed' at a Kilburn, North London, wedding was the £14,000 which an armed gang had just snatched from a supermarket round the corner.

And the 'something blue' was the thieves' language when their getaway car was caught up in the wedding traffic jam outside the church.

While they yelled and threatened, a woman guest calmly went on taking photographs of the bride and groom. And when robber Lee Baldwin leapt from the car in anger he, too, ended up in the picture.

Police had an easy job identifying him from the wedding snap. The blushing bride herself was not interested in a souvenir shot. Said she, 'These people could have ruined my happiest day.'

Hard-bitten case

It was unfortunate for shoplifter Maureen Colburn that the store she picked on had a former amateur Mr Universe as deputy boss. It wasn't all that wonderful an experience for him, either.

She finished in the dock and he ended up with a badly bitten backside.

Colburn was spotted stuffing a pillow case and jumper into her bag at a Bradford shopping centre. When stopped, the 19-year-old became demonstrative and hotly denied all knowledge of the theft. Enter assistant manager Bill Richardson, muscles rippling.

He hoisted her across his shoulders in a fireman's lift, whereupon she bit his bottom. Three times. In the general melee two security men and a brace of women store detectives had to retire injured while trying to restrain her.

'Eventually I had to sit on her,' Bill said.

Vanishing cream

All right then, how *does* one get rid of those unsightly blemishes which make one feel self-conscious?

Such was the problem facing 22-year-old Mark Keeling when he set forth on an armed robbery at a Feltham, Middlesex, electrical shop.

He was rightly worried that a rather gaudy tattoo of a swallow on his neck might give away his identity.

But wife Debbie was at hand with a solution. She covered the offending tattoo with a quick daub of her foundation cream.

That, plus a mask, should have done the trick. Unfortunately for Keeling, in the heat of the moment the cream vanished, clearly exposing the tell-tale swallow.

He was immediately identified and is now serving twelve years. The make-up artiste is on two years probation.

An 18-year-old girl accused of stealing a jar of vanishing cream has since disappeared, Huddersfield magistrate were told yesterday. – **Local Newspaper Report**

Crystal balls-up

A Dorset clairvoyant did not forsee the consequences when she gave a woman customer a duff fortune reading. The woman complained, and a Trading Standards officer made the short-sighted psychic hand back the fee.

Right villain

Irish shoplifter Seamus O'Brien didn't get anything right when he pinched two cowboy boots. Except for the boots themselves.

They were both right . . . right footed, that is.

One was a size nine, the other an 11. The size 11 was also stuffed full of cardboard. None of this seemed to bother O'Brien, who whipped off his worn out trainers and leapt into

the £29 boots.

Then he went on the run – well, on the limp actually – through Bedford town centre. He soon had the police hot on his high heels.

Bedford magistrates placed him on probation. And made him pay up for the useless footwear to boot.

* * *

John Markham was a bungling burglar who couldn't put a foot right either.

He smashed a car window and stole a bundle of women's clothing, but cut his hand so badly that police were able to follow the resulting trail of blood all the way back to his flat.

While questioning him about this and other sundry felonious occurrences police noticed that he was wearing two left-footed shoes, one of which still bore a price tag.

As a result of this discovery Markham was charged in connection with a raid on a shoe shop during which he managed to steal £15,000 worth of . . . yes, you guessed it . . . *left-footed* shoes.

Counter-feet

. . . And one can only presume a veritable gang of one-legged bandits was behind the smash and grab raid on Keith Scarrott's shop. They made off with a staggering £500 worth of odd shoes.

Lost soles

Asked to comment on thieves who had looted a shoe shop display rack, a police spokesman at Smethwick, West Midlands, said, 'They must be hopping mad.'

Their haul consisted of just 15 shoes. All right-footed.

Bandits at ten o'clock

While taking part in a massive NATO exercise over the Irish Sea, an RAF fighter pilot was alarmed to find a little Piper Cherokee on his wingtips.

The two men in it were considerably more exercised – they had £200,000 of smuggled cannabis on board.

As prosecutor Paul Chadd later told Gloucester Crown Court, 'They ran slap bang into the middle of the exercise and had the fright of finding an RAF Phantom, for all I know fitted with Sidewinders, alongside them.'

Into the bargain, the RAF pilot logged their 'plane's number and the pair had an unhappy landing at Bristol, where police were waiting to seize them.

Lost cause

The trio of masked desperadoes who tried a payroll heist at Greenhithe, Kent, had to call it a day when they could not find the wages department.

Pennies from heaven

Two New Yorkers picked the wrong day to go chasing money at gunpoint. Just around the corner they were giving the stuff away.

As they fled with their takings from a bank, the pair ran slap into a crowd of 5,000 people who were waiting for thousands of dollars to rain down from the Empire State Building.

In full view of a dozen TV cameras the two tried to push their way through. They were enthusiastically corralled by about 100 people after tripping themselves up on TV cables.

The dollars-from-heaven scheme, incidentally, was a publicity stunt to help promote adult education.

No, we didn't get the connection either.

Falling flat

In broad daylight two Kent men set out to steal a block of flats. A fairly substantial block, three storeys high and with some 60 rooms.

They carefully forged a contract, authorising them to demolish the building at Allhallows, near Gravesend.

Armed with the official-looking document they set to work, ripping out doors, floorboards and window frames.

They were having a smashing time until a curious bobby asked what they were doing. Whereupon the pair showed him their contract.

But they had made one small typing error, printing Allhallows as two words.

His suspicions aroused, the officer made further checks and discovered they were con-men.

By the time he returned to arrest them they had removed 116 floorboards, 17 steel window frames and 7 doors.

No hiding place

There was a thing on top of Leslie Brown's wardrobe and one night it went on the bleep. Bleep, bleep, bleep it went, and it just kept bleeping on and on.

Not that Leslie minded, for he couldn't hear it. But whizzing by, somewhere up in the stratosphere at 18,000 miles an hour, a satellite did.

And the message it got loud and clear from the thing on top of the wardrobe was Mayday . . . Mayday . . . Mayday . . .

Instantly an international rescue bid got off the ground. The Russians, who owned the satellite, alerted the British authorities.

An RAF Sea King helicopter was scrambled. Other services were on standby, fearing a major disaster. For hours the

BLEEBLE
BLEEBLE

chopper combed the target area off the west coast of Scotland.

Its tracking equipment began to pinpoint the source somewhere around Glasgow. Then the nearby town of Erskine. Then the neighbouring village of Rashieburn. And then, Brown's house.

Finally police homed in on top of his wardrobe – to a radar beacon stolen from a North Sea gas rig.

For reasons best known to itself, The Thing had suddenly developed a fault and started sending out distress calls. In the end it had to be smashed with a sledgehammer and thrown into the river Clyde to stop it bleeping.

It earned gas rig engineer Brown the distinction of being the first thief ever run to earth by a satellite.

Which must have come as small consolation to him when he was obliged to fork out a £500 fine and £1,599 compensation for all the bleeping nuisance he had caused.

A Multitude of Sins

And then there are the others. . . .

A Multitude of Sins

Elephantasia

Bored with making wine glasses eight hours a day, five days a week, Michael Jones took up a hobby in his lunch break.

He made glass elephants.

He made some for his wife. Then he made some for his friends. Then he made some more . . . and more and more. He made them for his wife to sell, but she couldn't get rid of them. And still Michael Jones kept turning out glass elephants.

They filled his mantlepiece, they crowded his cupboards. The house at Kingswinford, Worcestershire, was full of them.

In despair Mrs Eileen Jones began to dump them secretly in dustbins and in telephone kiosks. Soon glass elephants were turning up all over town.

Police finally tracked down the elephants' birthplace. There, Mrs Jones told them: 'He used to bring them home, one or two at a time.'

Explained Mr Jones: 'As far as I knew she was selling them. I didn't know she was throwing them away.'

Mr Jones, a prizewinning glassworker, lost his job. Because of the scandal he and his wife even had to move house. Said Mrs Jones: 'If anyone shows me another glass elephant I'll scream.'

Paw excuse

Mounties answering an alarm call at a bank in the Rocky Mountain resort of Jasper found a 7-ft black bear standing with its paws on the counter after crashing down the locked front door.

A thief went to work in the changing room at Burtonwood Rugby club. Honey was taken from the pockets of five players. – **Ashton and Haydock Reporter.**

Natural justice

Customs officers at London's Gatwick Airport were undeterred when a thorough search of three suspected drug smugglers revealed nothing.

They held the trio, two women and a seaman from Colombia, in Central America, for a few days, and let nature take its course.

Eventually the suspects yielded up 293 packets of cocaine in rubber condoms which they had swallowed.

The £224,000 haul was the largest ever smuggled internally into the UK.

One for the road

Londoner Fred Arnold did not touch a drop of beer in the barrel which rolled off the back of a lorry near Devizes, Wilts.

He explained to magistrates that he was a strict teetotaller and, as such, felt obliged to pour all the eighteen gallons of pale ale down the drain.

He then took the cask home, where his 15-year-old son sawed it in two as he wanted somewhere to keep his tadpoles.

Mr Arnold was ordered to pay for the barrel . . . and the beer.

Just desserts

It all started with a cream bun. The flavour hit Daniel Stratch in much the same way that Oliver Twist once found himself moved by porridge; in short, he wanted more.

Soon he had graduated to eclairs, strawberry shortcake, profiteroles and huge wedges of Black Forest gateau. His taste buds howled out for anything sweet, provided that it was also knee-deep in cream.

Daniel's habit was an expensive one to maintain. Sometimes, when he had blown all his money, he would spend his lunch-break in an agony of window shopping around the local patisseries.

Then one day he discovered sour cream and cabbage. After that you could forget cherry pie, lemon souffle and boring old creme caramel. Daniel now saw them for what they were – mere trifles. Sour cream and cabbage was a magnificent obsession.

He took to lunchtime orgies in the delicatessens of Riez in the French Alps. He spent his coffee breaks slavering outside their windows. He spent his employer's time sniffing out fresh eating places.

The boss fired him but Daniel did not mind too much as work was getting in the way of his passion anyway. The trouble was that he could no longer afford to scoff pounds and pounds of sour cream and cabbage.

And so began his life of crime. At night, while the rest of Riez slept, he took to sneaking out of his humble attic. Then over the rooftops he crept until at last he found himself above the delicatessen.

He burgled them one after another, stealing nothing but vast amounts of sour cream and cabbage. And in every case he swallowed the evidence on the spot.

But Daniel quickly ran out of delis to loot. In desperation he turned to raiding the fridges of private homes, seeking only the cream of society.

The end came on one particularly successful sortie. Bloated and gorged with grub, Daniel fell asleep in a chair and was still there when the owners came home.

They reported he had been 'snoring gently and with a contented smile on his face.' The contentment rapidly vanished when the judge put Daniel on a two month cream-free diet – behind bars.

Alarming

The armed raid on a Shoreditch, London, Post Office was less than successful for the two perpetrators. Their total haul? . . . one burglar alarm.

Even More Alarming

And in Northampton, thieves broke into a car and stole its anti-theft device.

Profit and loss

Even less successful was the bandit who pulled a gun on unemployed Salvatore Gioiello in a Naples street and ordered him to hand over all his cash.

He squirmed with embarrassment as Salvatore burst into tears and cried, 'If only I could. I've been out of work for two years and I have a wife and three children who are always hungry.'

Shamefaced, the crook took a well-filled wallet from his pocket and, pressing it into Salvatore's trembling hand, told him: 'Don't cry. Take this.' Then he turned and walked away.

Guessing the wallet, and the 100,000 lire (about £40) it contained had been stolen, Salvatore took it to the local police station.

Three days later the owner called on Salvatore, gave him the 100,000 lire – 'For being so honest' – and promised to help find him a job.

The fate of the soft-hearted mugger is not recorded.

Saucy

Thieves who hopped it with 300 pairs of frogs' legs from a Chesham, Buckinghamshire, restaurant offended the good taste of French chef Daniel Piedvache. Said he 'What really annoys me is they forgot the sauce . . . and you can't serve frogs' legs without Sauce Provencale.'

Booty

When a Gloucester man was fined £10 for stealing-by-finding a suitcase which fell from a car, Douglas Smith, the suitcase's owner, paid up instead.

Handing the court ten £1 notes, Mr Smith explained: 'My wife says I should be in the dock for having a faulty boot lock and putting temptation in people's way.'

Leaving the court the defendant said: 'That was the act of a good Samaritan.'

Something borrowed

Bride-to-be Linda Mighell kept a fashion shop assistant busy in the fitting room while her fiance made off with a £129 wedding dress.

Jailed for four months, Linda told Southend magistrates: 'I wanted a white wedding but I couldn't afford one, so we decided to go out and steal the dress.'

Her fiance – now her husband – was remanded for reports.

Curses

On having a gun poked into his tummy by a teenage crook, insurance salesman Alfred Rout, 63, told him: 'F . . . OFF!' The teenager duly effed off and Mr Rout was praised by Judge Michael McMullan for his courage.

Parking lot

It seems there are many citizens in New York who are more than somewhat reluctant to cough up for their old parking tickets.

This is giving the authorities a big headache as they need

the folding stuff very badly. So one day they think up this racket whereby if your car is towed away by the boys in blue, you must pay these tickets before you get your transport back.

Naturally there are some persons who owe so much on tickets they do not think it is good business to pay out more than their car is worth.

So New York's finest start to auction off these unclaimed wheels and the City does very nicely from such transactions I'm told.

But George Popp who rides a motorbike does not think it very gentlemanly when the Mayor sends him a bill for £1,800 just so he can get back on two wheels again.

He is especially unhappy as the officers unhitch his bike from a fire hydrant where he says it causes nobody any heart-ache.

This Popp character does not care much for the Mayor's idea but he does not tell the Mayor. Instead he goes along to the auction and he buys back his buzz-about for £160.

The way he figures it, he does very prosperously out of the proceedings. He does not pay any scratch for this fine or any other.

Personally, I am thinking maybe Popp is a very smart guy indeed.

(With apologies to Damon Runyon)

A youth who stole more than £500 worth of goods from a school was fined £40 at Edinburgh Sheriff Court.

Roy Allen, 19, of 61a Woodburn Park, Dalkieth, admitted breaking into Dalkieth High School on January 6 and stealing two language masters, a number of musical instruments and other items. – **Evening News** Report

Last laugh

The two Chelsea burglars had to laugh. And who, indeed, could blame them?

There they were, all alone in this very tasty residence, swag all around them and, on the floor before them, a whole heap of children's comics.

They began to read and, 'ere long, forgot all about the true purpose of their mission, which had to do with wall safes and antique silver and such like.

How they tittered. How they laughed. How time flew. An hour passed in this happy fashion as the pair lay on the first floor landing chortling away.

It was in this unlikely position that they were found by a young woman and her cousin looking after the house while its owners were abroad.

Pausing only to wipe the smiles off their faces, the burglars fled, leaving behind a suitcase of valuables. Their entire haul? – a fiver and an old cheque book!

Scales of justice

Pandemonium reigned in the courtroom in Mombasa, Kenya, when a giant Monitor lizard standing over 3 ft high in its fighting stance, and a ferocious carnivore if ever there was one, wandered into the middle of a trial. During the panicked exodus of court officials, spectators and police, the unfortunate reptile was savagely beaten to death with chairs and benches, but not before 20 criminal suspects had made good their escape.

Rich port

As she downed her glass of port in a Nottingham pub, a woman customer was astonished to find a diamond ring in her mouth.

The ring had been placed in the glass for safekeeping by the publican's wife while she did some cleaning.

It was later recovered from the customer's husband, who was fined for stealing it.

Short circuit

Faced with redundancy, electrician Gerald Millen switched to a career of crime. It lasted just two hours.

On his first burglary the owner spotted him half in and half out of a window. When challenged, Millen said: 'I'm a burglar,' waved, and ran away.

On his second attempt, a few doors down along the same street at Camberley, Surrey, he was disturbed by the lady of the house coming home, despite having bolted the front door on his way in.

When confronted, Millen broke down in tears. He showed her he had not taken anything, begged her forgiveness, and asked for five minutes to get away.

But as he fled he ran straight into the arms of police investigating the first raid.

Action replay

The aggrieved Irishman had no real grounds to lodge a claim for damages. His lawyer, Geoffrey Cohen, told him so.

But the Cardiff solicitor also told him: 'In fairness you may be best advised to take a second opinion.'

And so that very afternoon the Irishman phoned him again . . . to ask for a second opinion.

CLASS
by Jilly Cooper

CLASS IS DEAD! Or so everyone claims. Who better to refute this than Jilly Cooper!

Describing herself as 'upper middle class', Jilly claims that snobbery is very much alive and thriving! Meet her hilarious characters! People like Harry Stow-Crat, Mr and Mrs Nouveau-Richards, Samantha and Gideon Upward, and Jen Teale and her husband Brian. Roar with laughter at her horribly unfair observations on their everyday pretensions – their sexual courtships, choice of furnishings, clothes, education, food, careers and ambitions. . .

For they will all remind you of people that you know!

'Highly entertaining, acerbic and wickedly observant . . . certain to become as much part of the verbal shorthand as was Nancy Mitford's *U and Non-U* a generation ago'
The Economist

'Enormously readable and very funny'
Cosmopolitan

0 552 11525 8   £2.50

JOLLY MARSUPIAL
Down Under And Other Scenes
by Jilly Cooper

More infectious humour and witty observations from Jilly
Cooper, whose latest collection of articles, originally published in *The Sunday Times* and the *Mail on Sunday*,
includes a light-hearted and irreverent account of a visit to
Australia, published for the first time in its entirety. Scenes
nearer home, viewed with equal disrespect include the
diverse worlds of a vet's conference, fashionable charity
balls, the London to Brighton run and Hen Night in Wands-
worth. And, as always, Jilly Cooper is a devastating, hilarious and sometimes moving chronicler of the minutiae of
family life, with some fascinating sidelights and side-swipes
at the middle-class educational rat race along the way.

This new set of writings will prove once again Jilly Cooper's
ability to provoke, fascinate and – above all– amuse!

0 552 12359 5   £1.75

SUPER JILLY
by Jilly Cooper

Here's our famously zany social commentator on top form once again! This collection of Jilly Cooper's witty anecdotes includes 'Paws', the tale of her dreadful dog, a hazardous visit to Harrods' sales and a hilarious account of judging a well-dressed turkey competition!

Whether interviewing Mrs Thatcher, lunching with the mums of today's Debs, or defining the magic of 'machismo' Jilly's acerbic wit and shrewd observations make SUPER JILLY an entertaining and provocative read.

0 552 11802 8   £1.25

ANY FOOL CAN BE A COUNTRYMAN
by James Robertson

After pig farming there was a dairy farming, and after dairy farming James Robertson thought he'd try his hand at running a bed and breakfast house in an old mill, and sometimes inside the mill too. There was also Bill, who padded round the garden at night with a shotgun, looking for Hitler. There were shoots where the visitors fell into slurry pits and the pheasants sat and watched. There were hunts where a corpse followed the hounds in a Land Rover. There were irate farmers, village rows, ramblers, drunks, warlocks and cricket matches.

And at the end of it all James Robertson decided that people were just as peculiar as pigs and cows, and that he had at last become a full blown countryman.

0 552 12560 1   £1.75

ANY FOOL CAN BE A PIG FARMER
by James Robertson

Cats, dung and overdrafts are the three things you can be sure of finding on every farm. But on James Robertson's farm there were also rats, bats, and a boa constrictor. And of course there were the pigs . . .

Sow Number Seven, Queen of the Pen and winner of all the porcine gang wars.

George, who was supposed to father piglets on all the tribe, but fell in love with Number Eleven and wore all the hair from her back.

Duke, whose idea of being sexy was to come galumphing up and take a jump at the sow of his choice. As he weighed the best part of a ton several promising romances were squashed until he was put on a diet.

James Robertson was kicked, bitten, piddled on, and infected wit pig lice. But he survives and lives to tell the tale in *Any Fool Can Be a Pig Farmer*.

0 552 12399 4   £1.75

JOLLY SUPER
by Jilly Cooper

Jilly Cooper is a household name. She is read and discussed all over the world – her postbag bulges with approving and disapproving letters. She delights some people with her witty comments on day-to-day life, problems and people, and she irritates others beyond belief.

Here is a chance to read again some of her most famous pieces. Whether she is coping with uninvited guests, going hunting, describing her favourite fads and fancies, or merely reporting on the scene around her, her articles are full of laughter laced with good common sense. The ideal Jilly Cooper reader says: 'That's just what I've always been thinking – but I wouldn't have dared to admit it.'

0 552 11751 X   £1.25

JOLLY SUPERLATIVE
by Jilly Cooper

More witty words and caustic comments from the witheringly funny Jilly Cooper!

With her insatiable love of puns and her vivid response to people and places, *Jolly Superlative* includes more hilarious happenings in the life of Jilly Cooper – such as the revolt of the Putney Common dogwalkers and a trip to Butlins with 450 vicars! Jilly comments on adultery, suburban snobbery and the sexual rites of professional-class society – as well as the hilarities, horrors and joys of life.

0 552 11801 X   £1.25

HOORAY FOR YIDDISH!
by Leo Rosten

Here is the rich, colourful and gloriously irreverent world of
Yiddish and the riotous English that came out of it, the only
language that answers a question with a question: 'Does this
book have jokes?' 'Does this book have *jokes*!'

Diner: You call this meat?
Waiter: What's wrong with it?
Diner: It tastes funny.
Waiter: So laugh.

And you will.

Garnished with stories, jokes, parables, epigrams, acerbi-
ties and Talmudic insights, *Hooray for Yiddish!* takes us on
illuminating side-trips into the faith, folklore, tradition and
genius, history and language of the Jewish people. When
you finish – and you will never really finish, for this is a
book to dip into again and again – you will be speaking Yiddish like a native. So enjoy!

'One of the best collections of Jewish jokes around'
Time Out

0 552 12532 6   £3.95

THE BOOK OF NARROW ESCAPES
by Peter Mason
Illustrated by McLachlan

'So there I was, hurtling hysterically earthwards at 185 miles an hour, head down, with a useless rip-cord tightly clenched in my white-knuckled fist, with roughly ten seconds to live . . .'

It may – or may not – have been at this point that author Peter Mason came up with the bestselling idea of *The Book of Narrow Escapes*. What is certain is that he has gathered together some of the most hilarious, mind-boggling and spine-chilling brushes with death, the law and all sorts of other forces outside our normal control of this brilliantly illustrated volume.

The Book of Narrow Escapes is a highly amusing, and occasionally terrifying collection of what might have been if the gods of luck had been looking the other way.

0 552 12436 2   £1.50

A SELECTION OF HUMOROUS BOOKS AVAILABLE
FROM CORGI BOOKS

While every effort is made to keep prices low, it is sometimes necessary to increase prices at short notice. Corgi Books reserve the right to show new retail prices on covers which may differ from those previously advertised in the text or elsewhere.

The prices shown below were correct at the time of going to press.

☐ 99052 3	**CYNICS DICTIONARY (B format)**	*Russell Ash*	£2.50
☐ 99012 4	**INTELLIGENT AND LOYAL (B format)**	*Jilly Cooper*	£2.50
☐ 11525 8	**CLASS**	*Jilly Cooper*	£2.50
☐ 12359 5	**JOLLY MARSUPIAL**	*Jilly Cooper*	£1.75
☐ 11832 X	**SUPER COOPER**	*Jilly Cooper*	£1.25
☐ 11801 X	**JOLLY SUPERLATIVE**	*Jilly Cooper*	£1.25
☐ 11802 8	**SUPER JILLY**	*Jilly Cooper*	£1.25
☐ 11751 X	**JOLLY SUPER**	*Jilly Cooper*	£1.25
☐ 11752 8	**JOLLY SUPER TOO**	*Jilly Cooper*	£1.25
☐ 12624 1	**THE LITTLE BLACK BOOK**	*J. J. Gabay*	£1.50
☐ 12685 3	**DESERT ISLAND BIFF**	*Chris Garratt & Mick Kidd*	£2.95
☐ 12436 2	**THE BOOK OF NARROW ESCAPES**	*Peter Mason*	£1.50
☐ 12622 5	**TOTALLY TASTELESS GRAFFITI**	*Hugh Mungus*	£1.50
☐ 12681 0	**IT'S DIFFERENT IN THE COUNTRY**	*Liz Potter*	£1.75
☐ 12560 1	**ANY FOOL CAN BE A COUNTRYMAN**	*James Robertson*	£1.75
☐ 12399 4	**ANY FOOL CAN BE A PIG FARMER**	*James Robertson*	£1.75
☐ 12532 6	**HOORAY FOR YIDDISH (B format)**	*Leo Rosten*	£3.95
☐ 12402 8	**FANNY PECULIAR**	*Keith Waterhouse*	£1.95

ORDER FORM

All these books are available at your book shop or newsagent, or can be ordered direct from the publisher. Just tick the titles you want and fill in the form below.

CORGI BOOKS, Cash Sales Department, P.O. Box 11, Falmouth, Cornwall.

Please send cheque or postal order, no currency.

Please allow cost of book(s) plus the following for postage and packing:

U.K. Customers—Allow 55p for the first book, 22p for the second book and 14p for each additional book ordered, to a maximum charge of £1.75.

B.F.P.O. and Eire—Allow 55p for the first book, 22p for the second book plus 14p per copy for the next seven books, thereafter 8p per book.

Overseas Customers—Allow £1.00 for the first book and 25p per copy for each additional book.

NAME (Block Letters) ....

ADDRESS ....

....